FRENCH CATHEDRALS

FRENCH CATHEDRALS

MARTIN HÜRLIMANN

JEAN BONY

DESCRIPTIVE NOTES BY PETER MEYER

A Studio Book · THE VIKING PRESS · New York

FIRST PUBLISHED BY ATLANTIS VERLAG AG ZURICH 1951
FIRST ENGLISH EDITION 1951
REPRINTED 1954
NEW EDITION 1961
NEW REVISED EDITION © 1967 THAMES AND HUDSON LIMITED, LONDON
PUBLISHED IN 1967 BY THE VIKING PRESS, INC.
625 MADISON AVENUE, NEW YORK, N. Y. 10022
PRINTED AND BOUND IN GERMANY

CONTENTS

INTRODUCTION Page 7

MAP SHOWING LOCATION OF CATHEDRALS Page 33

FRENCH CATHEDRALS

JUST as the Greek temple is simple both in form and in function, so the Gothic cathedral seems to proclaim the complexity of mankind and of the world. Like the Celestial Jerusalem of which it is the terrestrial image, it contains in its bosom many mansions, which it is the mission of architecture to arrange in a clear order and to bind together within broad perimeters: for the cathedral summons men from far and wide, with its belfries, its façades: and the manifold approaches of its portals. Its very shape seems to be modelled on the movement of the crowds whose steps and glances it holds in focus; and the vast space it encloses is fully defined only by the sonorous volume of its organ and the songs that echo in its depths. Without its ritual and its people, the cathedral would lose much of its significance; yet it would retain its cosmic quality, its rich quality of meditation upon the facts of the universe. For with masterly skill it exploits and organizes substance and weight, space and light, just as it does the masses of humanity; and in the multiplicity of the rhythms with which it links them, in the movements that it combines and blends together, it seems to identify itself with the fundamental impulses of the mind and of nature.

This magnificent framework that architecture provides is only one element of the artistic effort represented by these gigantic structures. The stained glass windows assemble in their translucent lights the richest effects of colour and outline of which an almost inexhaustible iconography is capable; and the ubiquitous sculpture, aligned in strands of foliage, in rows of capitals adorned with traceries of plants, and in series after series of figures portrayed with an extraordinary freedom of expression, is mustered against the façades in huge compositions whose richness and vitality on the human plane is matched by the majesty of their spiritual content. This wonderful florescence is all the more astonishing when one recalls that, at the time these cathedrals were built, human dwellings, even those of noblemen, were still of a rustic simplicity. The cathedral was the only place where all forms of art could be developed.

There is no doubt that the Romanesque abbeys had already prepared the way for these splendours. By opening their doors to crowds of pilgrims they had already brought about a synthesis of human activities. But they continued to serve their monastic purpose, to adhere to the rigid time-table of offices sung hour by hour in a rhythm foreign to secular life; and at intervals reformers would recall them to their vows of poverty and spiritual renunciation. The first half of the twelfth century resounded with the vehement objurgations of St Bernard; but whilst condemning, in the monastic churches, the vain splendours of imagination as harmful to a spirituality whose duty was to practise pure contemplation, he none the less recommended the employment, in churches intended for the faithful, of images that would strike the eye. It is the duty of cathedrals, those churchly mothers of ancient cities, to exploit all the glories of art, and to present to men's eyes pictorial lessons such as can at need supplement the teaching of theological truths. It is certainly not a matter of chance that the flowering of the great cathedrals coincided with the spreading of Cistercian austerity, especially in view of the fact that it came to an end when the growth of a lay clientele had begun to make an increasing claim upon artists' activities. During the interval, of little more than a century, between these two developments, it was the old city cathedrals that concentrated all creatively artistic effort and thus, thoroughly rebuilt, became the symbol of a civilization in full flower.

Despite the inevitable overstatement involved in such simplifications, it can be said that the Gothic cathedral sums up a whole epoch of humanity; that in these cathedrals a social structure, a theological mode of thought, together with a long tradition of craftsmanship and sensibility, found their most beautiful and most human expression. And this explains the fascination they have for the soul of modern man.

But this important historical development, which has affected the whole meaning we give to the word 'cathedral', so that it is now synonymous with 'Gothic', did not take place diffusely throughout western Europe. It occurred in a particular region of twelfth-century France, in that collection of territories, grouped around Paris, which have come to be known as the Ile de France although it spreads out into the neighbouring provinces and extends over Picardy, Champagne, and Berry in the south, and to the west as far as Maine. It need therefore be no cause for surprise that this volume does not concern itself either with the Romanesque cathedrals, which were anterior to this development, nor with those that emphasize the regional features of Gothic art, such as the cathedrals of Angers or Albi. We have taken care never to move very far away from the original centres of Gothic art: we have laid the stress on the great classic works and, restricting our survey to the northern half of France, have selected Normandy, so close to Paris on the map, as our choice example of the provincial variants of Gothic, while Strasbourg, so close to Champagne in its style, is the only reminder of the wider and somewhat later expansion of the styles born in the Ile de France.

This concentration of theme, if it reduces the area, nevertheless increases the scope of this study; for it is around Paris, Chartres, Amiens, and Rheims that the destiny of Gothic art is decided, in sculpture as well as in architecture. It is in this region that the maximum of richness is combined with the maximum of cohesion, and it is on the cathedrals of these four cities, the most classic of them all, that this volume lays special emphasis. The reader is thus presented, not with a more or less haphazard collection of buildings with nothing in common except their title of cathedral, but with a genuine grouping of works that are closely linked both geographically and in time. Without disregarding either the picturesque or the historically unexpected, we have sought to draw a lesson from these illustrations and to make them express the development of Gothic art in the very place where it sprang up.

Remarkable alike for their stature, for the singleness of their conception, and for the richness of their stained glass windows and sculptures, the cathedrals of the Ile de France have for more than a century been the object of an almost fanatical admiration. What the Romantics especially noticed about them was their seeming disorder: the imagination of these people delighted in the abundance of all the later additions, made over a period of centuries, to the original structure. Nowadays we are less appreciative of this poetry of chance, and our minds are more concerned with the principles of order that govern the cunning construction of these buildings. Viollet-le-Duc, whose keenness of eye and analytical method were both worthy of admiration, although his ideas of engineering were more questionable, succeeded in tracing the evolution of French Gothic down to the last detail, reducing the subject to a sort of constructional theorem of which one needed only to study the development. It must be admitted that he went too far in this direction, and believed that he could detect a technical logic in matters where, in fact, considerations of another sort were involved. We no longer believe that the ribs effectively carry the vault, or that the clusters of shafts channel clearly distributed stresses to the ground. We no longer accept his theory of 'counter-braces', according to which detached shafts had greater resistance than the main masonry. The real forces of construction reside in the thickness of structures, and not in their surfaces.

Nevertheless it would be wrong to allow ourselves to react too strongly against Viollet-le-Duc's teachings; for as a rule it is enough merely to translate them into other terms in order to give them their full value. Those lines which he regards as performing the function of supports are certainly no more than a handwriting; but their design transcribes, with some freedom of interpretation, what is going on behind them, and express what was believed by the architects to be the theoretical framework of the building. There is better reason for reproaching Viollet-le-Duc for having misunderstood certain important aspects of architectural thought, for having laid too exclusive an emphasis upon functional logic and having thus presented a picture of French Gothic that was too sterile and too uniform. It is true that French architecture of the twelfth century was careful always to create systems of forms that could be justified by reason, and that it eschewed indulgence in pure fantasy. But architects still had a wide field of initiative left open to them: that of the arrangement of proportions, planes and masses, and all the art of silhouettes, of those motifs and rhythms of supports and openings which give a building its own character. With the result that nowadays we are less impressed by the quasi-mechanical regularity of the Gothic masters' system of construction than by the variety of their researches and the originality of their individual ideas.

Every cathedral has its own personality. That is because each is the work of one man, the one who designed it, or at the most of two or three masters in cases where the original plan was subjected to appreciable modifications in the course of building. The majority of these great men remain unknown. Only in the case of Amiens, which was undertaken by Robert de Luzarches; of Rouen; of Rheims, if it be true that Jean d'Orbais was its original architect; and of Notre-Dame de Paris, provided we are willing to give credit for its glory to the master mason Richard whose signature appears at the bottom of a document of the period, have we any record of their names.

But there must have been at that time in Paris many a prominent architect; and how are we ever to know the name of the master of Sens, of Laon, of Bourges, or Chartres? In many cases it is possible to detect the stamp of several personalities. At Notre-Dame de Paris, the nave is much more refined, much more elegant in its twelfth-century way than the choir, and the façade suggests yet another approach. At Noyon also, three masters must have worked in succession, each with his own style and highly individual characteristics. We can sometimes detect, without knowing his name, from what part of France the architect came: thus the choir at Le Mans was conceived and initiated by a man from the Soissonnais, but was continued ten years later by a Norman, perhaps the Thomas Toustain who is mentioned in a text dating from 1258, only four years after the dedication.

But after all, why worry about names, which convey little more than does complete anonymity, in the face of the finished work, so very much more revealing and more instructive than any text? It is the building which proclaims the prodigious imagination of the originators of Laon, of Bourges, or of Le Mans; the rigorous ordering of the minds of the Parisian masters; the breadth of vision of the architect of Chartres; the clarity of style of him who fashioned Rheims; the breath-taking audacity of the master of Beauvais. Each cathedral has its motifs and favourite themes. At Paris the main effect is that of cubes, arranged in solid, compact blocks; at Chartres the rose triumphs, at Rheims the pinnacle, at Le Mans the detached, almost self-contained chapel; at Bourges the chief emphasis is on the triforium, while a singular slenderness of forms constitutes another major motif; whereas Rheims, in spite of its elegance, is in fact more massive and more solid.

There remains, however, a logical bond which links together all these individual trends of thought; it is the line of evolution of style, the forward march of a singularly progressive architecture, which steadily advances from generation to generation. There can be no doubt that the influence of archæological classifications, which perhaps lay too much stress on the shape of the pillars and windows and the moulding of the profiles, has been responsible for the tendency to see in Gothic architecture a continuous evolution towards paring down the supporting piers and steadily extending the openings. Doubtless it is true, fundamentally true, that there was an irresistible urge in this direction, and that Gothic architecture owes its very particular tone to the new proportion it established between the solid masses and the ever-increasing voids, either open arcades or windowed surfaces.

It seems, however, that a little too much stress has been laid on the linear aspects of Gothic architecture and on the geometry which presides over the disposition of the networks of colonnettes and mouldings, of mullions and ribs. Too often the very essence of Gothic art has been taken to reside in the ultimate refinements of a web-like texture and in a kind of diagram drawn in the filigree of a hard stone, carved with that incisive elegance which is symptomatic of a highly elaborated style. This current view of the nature of Gothic art would place its zenith at the moment when it is losing its impetus, when the stature of the buildings tends to decrease and when the great edifices are nearly all finished.

This fact alone should be enough to make one sceptical of such an interpretation, for Gothic art defined itself through its great undertakings and must have been consciously following a clear-cut conception of its aims when wanting to enlarge them to such a super-human scale. Only, what it was then seeking was not linear subtlety. Its graphic representation was not an end in itself: it served to design and describe volumes, and it is to this art of handling space that the architecture of cathedrals owes its remarkable power.

It is only necessary to look at the oldest of Gothic naves, the nave of Sens, started before 1142 to realize that the whole effect of grandeur is produced by the amplitude of the interior volume, by the relatively great height of the aisles and still more by the colossal dimensions of the units of space, those vast cells, measuring more than 52 feet across, which the projecting piers carve out. In galleried churches such as Noyon, Laon, or Notre-Dame de Paris, the composition is quite different, the dominant rhythm being much smaller in scale; it is a tight pattern of cross-ruling which repeats series of similar elements at several levels and in several widths. But it still conforms to a system of tiers and juxtaposed volumes. And Notre-Dame de Paris owes its particular beauty to the contrast between the almost infinite multiplication of its small lateral cells, and the simplicity and extreme height of the central cavity which seems to be carved out of that surrounding mass constructed on so vastly different, and so far less bold a scale.

At Laon (Plate 164) and in the south transept of Soissons (Plate 167) one gets the impression of great width rather than of height; the volume of the central nave no longer appears channelled between high walls, but seems to spread laterally to such an extent that it penetrates deeply into the tiered galleries which flank it and surround it, as with a circular sweep, in the apse. This wide aeration contrasts sharply with the slender, brittle walls of the Parisian school, and confers on the interior space a supple play and a mobility of depth already to some extent anticipated in the choir of Noyon. But the structural frame remains the same, the weft of the elevations preserves the same tight texture, and it is at Soissons that the architecture of the end of the twelfth century attains its finest effects of differentiation and integration.

In the thirteenth century the language of architecture is transformed, following the invention of the flying buttress, which, in 1180, began to be introduced above the lateral roofs, and which gave so great an upward and outward freedom to the buildings. But it is still in terms of volumes, of expanses to be conquered that the builders of Chartres and Bourges, Rheims and Amiens, Le Mans and Beauvais, think. The proof lies in the very lay-out of their edifices.

At Chartres (Plates 48-49) a new kind of elevation appears in which the big arches on the lower level and the considerably enlarged clerestory windows counterbalance each other on either side of the horizontal belt of the triforium. This formula was to be adopted again in the naves of Soissons (Plate 166), Rheims (Plate 102), and Amiens (Plates 130 and 132) and most of the later Gothic churches up to the end of the Middle Ages. The reason is that it permits an extreme simplification of the arrangement of the nave: increased height for the vertical divisions, and a clear-cut sectioning of the interior space into two vast zones, one of which constitutes the aisles, extending it laterally, while the other rises alone into the heights, bounded by the luminous panels of the clerestory windows.

But the creative ability of the master of Chartres did not stop there: he also imposed on his building a tight rhythm of transverse divisions. For the groups of engaged columns, jutting firmly out and of truly voluminous dimensions, which rise vertically from the ground to the vault, not only serve to give to the nave an ascending movement; they are also meant to section it into a series of narrow compartments which seem compressed one against the other in rapid succession, and whose sharp divisions are taken up again outside by the large screen-work of the flying buttresses. It would be too easy to see in the flying buttress just a technical process: from this early period on it is used scientifically to delineate the exterior space which it penetrates deeply, and to stress the same transverse cuts which proportion out the space enclosed by the naves. There again, despite the novelty of the constructive solutions, we find ourselves in the presence of a concerted system which tends to express, above all, the laws of composition of built-up volumes.

Although exactly contemporary with Chartres, Bourges takes us into a totally different world (Plate 179). Here the accent is on the unity of the interior space and on a progressive development of the height. One passes successively from one really very low exterior aisle to a collateral one which already has the attributes of a nave, to arrive at last at the extreme height of the nave proper, whose elevation, suspended as it were above gigantic pillars, seems paradoxically to defy gravity. The repetition of the triforium motif only seems to accentuate this mounting by stages which carries upward the great disencumbered volume. One seeks in vain, in the effects of linear verticality of later periods, such a degree of power as is given to a building by deliberately envisaging every aspect from the point of view of volume; and however elegant may be the nave of Amiens, attenuated by having been drawn upwards, the resulting impression of lightness is certainly no stronger than in the nave of Bourges.

So far we have concentrated almost entirely on the interior of cathedrals; but their exterior is composed with the same mastery. From the solid, closed-in mass of Sens, one passes to the already more open surfaces of Noyon (Plate 155) or Laon (Plate 161), where the divisions remain smooth and even. The regular arrangement into three tiers forming one block with the non-projecting transept, gave to Notre-Dame de Paris from the outset a powerful and compact outline, which was not too seriously interfered with by the renovations undertaken during the second half of the thirteenth century. And it was from Notre-Dame that Bourges derived its inspiration in the matter of volume composition (Plate 180), though greater accent is already placed on the transverse planes of the flying buttresses. But at Rheims (Plate 58) we return to a straight vertical outline; the abutments of the flying buttresses rise directly up, surmounted by their tier of pinnacles and creating a high mesh of vertical shafts which encase the upward thrust of the central nave.

Beauvais (Plate 133) was but to accentuate both this height and this movement; whereas at Le Mans (Plate 150), which takes up again and enriches the formula of the chevet of Chartres, the composition of volumes becomes appreciably more complex. The flying buttresses, which multiply themselves by dividing into two half-way up, delineate more clearly than ever the framework of a spacious volume in the midst of which rises, in successive tiers, the central mass of the chevet. But they alone do not determine the main outline of the building; for below them is a last and even larger tier, composed of a complete ring of chapels which spread out fanwise and seem to emphasize the radial movement which has the choir as its hub. In this richness of movement, in this power of propagation, in this organized swelling of volumes there lies a very different beauty from that of Rheims or Beauvais. And no doubt it would be wrong to neglect the picturesque aspects of such a composition, the shadows which lie between the chapels, the facets of the buttresses. All these effects are, however, subordinate to one grand over-all vision, which determines that the sharpest lines shall serve only to demarcate and articulate the volumes.

We have still neglected many things: the play of the towers, the evolution which leads from the ancient spire of Chartres (Plate 11) to that of Senlis (Plate 157), the turning movement of the towers of Laon (Plates 154, 161-163), which seem to have been made to pivot on their square base, and to face in all directions. It is in this mobility of volumes that Laon fore-shadows thirteenth-century architecture. But Laon is also a kind of immense candelabrum set on a height, with its cluster of towers arranged in pairs around a powerful central lantern-tower; and it is here also that the Gothic façade was created.

Before Laon, the façades of the twelfth century were cut up, in Norman fashion, into vertical sections containing windows and panels of wall arcading, but all this on rugged and relatively barren surfaces. Typical examples are Senlis (Plate 158), the old part of the façade of Sens (Plate 168) and, even more sectioned, the ancient west front of Chartres (Plate 11), which is preserved below the rose window of the new work.

After Laon the revised formula is adopted everywhere. It directs that the west front shall be divided into two vast stories, the lower one encompassing the porches, the upper framing a great rose window. Without the example of Laon, the present-day façade of Notre-Dame de Paris (Plate 1) would not have been conceivable; and that is why we cannot attribute this grandiose frontispiece to the year 1160, or even 1180. The west front of Notre-Dame is contemporary with the naves of Chartres and Bourges; it cannot have been designed more than a year or two before 1200. It is given quite exceptional authority and strength by the rigour of its geometry—the geometry not of a two-dimensional drawing, but of enormous blocks and dense and compact volumes which seem to assemble themselves irresistibly into the rigid form of a vast square. As for the recession of the façade above the 'Galerie des Rois' and again above the open-work arcading, a recession which is determined by the presence of a system of passages at the top of each of the blocks, it is this feature that gives to the design of the masses its vigorous clarity and, by fitting the tiers into each other, imparts to the whole composition that tranquil stability which gives satisfaction to the eye and to the mind.

In the thirteenth century an effort is made to establish a stricter correspondence between the façades and the interior elevation of the naves. Rheims is the finest example of the application of this principle, not so much to its west front, where the original plans have been slightly altered, but to the façades of the two transepts (Plate 88). Amiens (Plate 109), on the other hand, clearly demonstrates the contradictions architects were liable to run up against in this type of design; for the higher the nave, the greater became the distance between the rose window and the porches below, neither of which lend themselves to elongation. So it became necessary at Amiens to have recourse to two intermediate galleries: a triforium, as in the nave, and above it, as a stop-gap, the 'Galerie des Rois'. With the result that the slenderest and most delicate of Gothic naves (Plate 132) is preceded by a façade over-endowed with horizontal zones and decorative motifs.

Bourges (Plate 171), with its five porches corresponding to the five aisles of the nave, is another, rather exceptional, variation on the theme of the 'classic' Gothic front; but the modifications to which it was subjected at the end of the fourteenth and the beginning of the fifteenth centuries have partly obscured the forceful structures of the original.

It is only after 1240 that we see French Gothic give up these grand ventures, this ambitious experimentation with the form of volumes and the configuration of interior space. The meaning and tone of architecture suddenly change: and in spite of an ostensible fidelity to the formulæ of the preceding generation, a new era begins, a new type of Gothic, whose interest lies elsewhere. The *style rayonnant* already heralds the art of the late Middle Ages. Little is needed to upset all values which have hitherto pertained: it is only necessary to omit, on the outside, the cornices which define the volumes on the upper side. Inside, it is only necessary to open up the triforium (Plates 130 and 170) which, by its shape, had previously rendered articulate the vertical development of the elevation; or, again, to pare down the engaged columns to a point where they possess no more than a purely graphic quality, and to deprive them of that vigour which enabled them to jut like a wedge into the open space of the nave and to carve it into massive, clearly defined units. This absence of firm outlining blurs the surfaces, which take on the character of lace hangings. We have a premature example of this in the façade of Rheims (Plate 51), where the texture is subtle, mobile, and possessed of an extremely delicate and sensitive charm, but which lacks structural definition since the tiers tend to run one into the other, and which seems already on the way towards a kind of Gothic rococo.

At Notre-Dame de Paris (Plate 2) the casing is plainer, more rational, elegant in the style of a fine parchment drawing, but a loss of actual weight of material has been accompanied by a loss of spatial values. It is true that Viollet-le-Duc's restorations have given to the façades of the transept an appearance of fretwork which they did not originally possess; it is true that he carried still further the process of whittling down solid forms by modifying the windows of the choir galleries and giving them gables; but from the days of Jean de Chelles and Pierre de Montreuil, those concerned with Gothic were no longer thinking in terms of volumes, but seeking only slenderness and immateriality.

Where the naves were particularly high they did not lend themselves so readily to such disembodiment, and here and there one sees vigorous conceptions revived: at Châlons-sur-Marne (Plate 165) the opening-up of the triforium does not prevent the nave from achieving a beautiful plenitude of forms. But already in the choirs of Troyes and Amiens, an impression of fragility has been deliberately cultivated, while the choir of Evreux (Plate 153) shows how far this tendency had gone even before 1300. No better example could be imagined than the late thirteenth-century façade of Strasbourg Cathedral (Plate 182), where a maze of delicate forms in several layers of openwork masks and nullifies the solidity of the structure beneath, with a richness of inflections in which a Rhenish idiom can already be recognized.

This history of one and a half centuries is the history of the Ile de France and the regions immediately under its influence; it is not the history of the majority of French provinces, where Gothic art was the result of early and repeated importations, and where new principles had to adapt themselves to surviving traditions, often undergoing considerable alteration in the process.

Although very close geographically to Chartres and Paris, Normandy goes its own way; but it cannot altogether escape the influence of the Ile de France, and this influence complicates the evolution of its architecture. Generally speaking, it remains faithful to certain traits inherited from the Romanesque period; it retains the lantern-tower, abandoned by the Ile de France as early as 1200; it continues to erect very thick walls, which frame windows with deep arching, and which by their very weight, render unnecessary the development of the flying buttress (Plate 144); it seldom uses the French-style triforium, and prefers to retain its traditional clerestory passage permitting circulation round the very base of the windows. Lastly, it seems uninterested in those soaring ventures into space which are the glory of cathedrals in the grand tradition.

During the first half of the thirteenth century, Normandy is especially remarkable for richness of detail, for spandrels carved or ornamented with small sunken roundels, for luxurious mouldings which magnify the play of shadow and light. The interior elevation, with its high gallery-like triforium and its very small windows, keeps up the tradition of churches of the twelfth century. In all its features the choir of Bayeux (Plate 145) is closely akin to English architecture of the period, illustrating a trend which is found in many other buildings, in particular at Sées and the Mont St Michel.

Nevertheless, at the same time, in the region of the lower Seine valley, contacts with the Ile de France are closer. Rouen Cathedral adopts from Laon its seven-towered silhouette, from Chartres its three façades and, in the choir, an elevation directly inspired by the Soissonnais. The design of the chevet with three detached chapels remains poor and seems to repeat, merely enlarging it, a plan which is still quite Romanesque.

Apart from Rouen, Normandy is content, in general, with buildings of a moderate size; but little by little the influence of the Ile de France is more directly felt and the treatment of interior space alters completely. The nave of Bayeux (Plate 145) erects, on a tier of Romanesque arcades, immense windows which make the vault stand out very high, and which necessitate very powerful buttressing outside. But it is above all Coutances which, a little before the middle of the century, undertakes the construction of a choir inspired directly by Bourges and Le Mans (Plates 147-148), a choir whose spatial magnificence, although on a reduced scale, is by no means inferior to its prototypes.

Coutances also renews the old theme of the lantern-tower, by adopting an octagonal form (Plate 149) which recalls the Spanish *cimborios*, and by masking the complexity of its interior structure under an arrangement in one immense storey, flanked by thin corner turrets of surprising boldness (Plate 146). The façade, of only slightly earlier date, has the same up-thrusting power, and the same fineness of structure. But it must not be forgotten that Coutances, or at least, what is of importance at Coutances—the choir, the lantern-tower, and the façade —belongs to the middle of the century. It is contemporary in conception with the early *style rayonnant* of the Ile de France, of Picardy, or of Champagne; contemporary with Beauvais or the choir of Amiens. And to return to Bayeux, its nave obviously belongs to the second half of the century. This suffices to mark the disjointed chronology of styles which becomes apparent as soon as one leaves the original centre of Gothic art.

These provincial centres tend to lose their influence about the year 1300. At the very end of the century there is still a Norman variety of the *style rayonnant*, as shown by the transept of Bayeux, with its cluster of sunken roundels ~~string of small rose windows~~ filling all the spandrels along the walls; but from this time onwards the master mason Jean Davy was erecting at Rouen the façades of a transept conceived in the most orthodox and fully developed *style rayonnant*. These façades of Rouen can serve, with the choir of Evreux, to symbolize the diffusion throughout the whole of France of an architecture as uniform as the newly born monarchic administration.

In the following two centuries, work is not begun on any new great cathedrals in the northern half of France, apart from Nantes, erected at the zenith of ducal power; but everywhere there are buildings to be finished or to be altered to the style of the day.

The fourteenth century sees some important constructions: at Auxerre the nave, at Nevers the choir, at Le Mans the admirable south transept, whose gigantic windows, mounted on a base of twelfth-century walls, retain such a firm pattern (Plate 151). But the great creative movement is over: the cathedrals of northern France had nearly all been reconstructed during

PROPRIETES-FONDS DE COMMERCE

the two previous centuries and even where they remained unfinished, as at Troyes, work no longer progressed at the same rate; wars hold things in check, and it will take two centuries to finish a nave which in the thirteenth century would have been completed in twenty-five years. For the rest, we find only relatively unimportant additions: at Chartres, the St Piat chapel; at Rouen, the side chapels of the nave; at Amiens, the top of the south tower, the great end window of the north transept, and, here too, chapels down the sides of the nave; at Bourges, at the end of the century, that vast window is built into the centre of the west front, known as 'Le Grand Housteau' (Plate 171).

All the same, the last twenty years of the fourteenth century witness an important stylistic evolution: the *style flamboyant* appears at Rouen Cathedral, on a screen-like façade, strewn with statues in the English fashion (Plate 136). The central part of this west front was rebuilt in the sixteenth century, in the richest and most ornate *style flamboyant;* but on both sides, between the great central window and the towers, the panels topped by gables treated in open-work fashion and carrying square turrets with sharp little steeples, display the beginnings of the style with an elegance and a finesse still very much in the spirit of the fourteenth century. The west front of Rouen is not the only early example of the *style flamboyant;* there are also the west chapels of the nave of Amiens Cathedral and the Duc de Berry's addition to his palace at Poitiers. The sources of the style are complex, and it would be wrong to reduce them to the sole influence of English Decorated. Even before 1300, France had known, at the same time as England and in the same circles close to the court, the first symptoms of the new line of designs. More examples could perhaps be found in miniatures, ivories, and tombs, than in architecture proper; but these experiments were short-lived, neither flourishing nor developing to any extent. Later, there is an undeniable Germanic influence in certain shapes of columns. At Rouen, on the other hand, as indeed at Amiens, the imitation of certain English trends is obvious: at Rouen it is the screen-like façade mentioned above, at Amiens the star-shaped vaults; and it is understandable that Normandy and Picardy, both long closely linked with England, should have been the channels in France for influences from England.

Many cathedrals bear the mark of this *style flamboyant* which delights in fanciful curvilinear patterns, highly picturesque carved and moulded facings, and is characterized by a certain general lack of vigour in its forms. At Troyes the nave (Plate 170), although mostly fifteenth century, keeps the rigidity of the *rayonnant;* on the other hand, in Normandy the 'Tour de Beurre', the principal porch of the cathedral at Rouen and the north transept at Evreux (Plate 152) show the final outcome of this style. But richness is not always the keynote in these late developments of Gothic: there were also less ornate buildings, such as the west front of Nantes. What can be observed there is a tendency to return to massive structures, bearing the same weight of material, but lacking the clarity of composition which was the hall-mark of the great Gothic epoch. For the lines of this façade conform to no rule of volume distribution, and could be shifted without causing any fundamental change in either the structure, or indeed the general effect. The arbitrariness of linear play in *flamboyant* art is all the more apparent when the mural masses regain their fullness and their solidity; and it is doubtless thus that the final form assumed by Gothic in some measure paved the way for certain characteristics of Baroque architecture.

However much these late variations, brought about by this or that addition, may have altered the outward appearance of the great earlier buildings, the fact remains that the beauty of the cathedrals does not reside in this accidental picturesqueness. Their beauty is of quite a different order, for it is derived primarily from the great controlling thoughts of the twelfth- and thirteenth-century masters, from the exact design of each element of the building and from the way in which great numbers of those elements are reduced to a unity of precise and simple forms. Through splendid, novel, and varied use of space and of solid masses the Ile de France triumphed for more than a century over all other western countries, and it has remained one of the fountain-heads of architecture.

This implies, basically, great advances of technique: conquest of height, but also of breadth by the extension of the aisles and their chapels, by increasing the lateral depth; the Ile de France aimed in fact to enlarge space itself and to enrich it in every possible way. But this ever-increasing brilliance needed a firm purpose and a sense of spatial form. It is this all-embracing vision, this ability to master unerringly such enormous and complex masses, this superior strategy in architecture, which frequently leaves us almost dumbfounded. And although the mysterious effect which space has over us is not always a conscious one, it has secured for French cathedrals the admiration of the contemporary world. That admiration has also been evoked by the splendour of their sculptured decoration, and it is with this that the next section of our introduction deals.

★   ★   ★

Gothic sculpture is an integral part of the building: it is rigorously kept in the place which architecture reserves for it, but at the same time it brings to life the lines and surfaces of that architecture. It is no uneven partnership, but an understanding in which each serves the other, and Gothic art owes much of its charm to the constant fusion of the plastic and the monumental.

Architecture seeks to create, by the use of the great decorative techniques—sculpture and stained glass—strong, large-scale forms with which to obtain very powerful effects. Porches gain significance not only by being multiplied, but by the addition of porticos which, as at Chartres (Plates 29 and 40), meet the eye first and increase the total depth of the décor: at Notre-Dame de Paris, as early as 1200, they grow to gigantic proportions occupying half the total height of the naves and presenting a wide range of decorative form. Amiens and Rheims inherit this great size, which becomes typical of French Gothic of the thirteenth century. But the principle underlying these greatly amplified doors is seen also in the composite window of Chartres, and in the immense rose windows which, ever since Laon, have been set in terminal walls of the central aisle and of the transepts: further vast composite forms which place the whole of architecture at the service, this time, of stained glass.

Carving, on the other hand, is introduced into all the interstices of the structure; running in plant-like cordons along the line of demarcation of the storeys, carried round the arches of windows and clinging everywhere, in the axis of the abutments, in the spandrels, on the pointed ends of gables and down their sides, and even stretching along the sides of windows and the long openings of towers. The west front of Notre-Dame de Paris is marked by crockets which emphasize the lines of the arches, and has vigorous foliated cornices running across it (Plate 1); but it is at Laon (Plate 163), in particular, and a little later at Amiens (Plate 109), that this rich décor multiplies its motifs and varies by the mobility of its relief the key lines and the telling points of architecture. At Rheims the chevet itself (Plate 58) is decorated with a host of statues which accentuate the points of support, while softening the rather rigid lines. From 1250 there are more and more examples of over-indulgence in the use of sculptured décor, which tends to leave no plain surfaces and to oust the proper substance of architecture; but this represents an over-development in the later stages of an art which has already passed beyond its classical forms. For the Gothic of the great period is characterized by its precision, and by the discipline which controls the development of each technique.

All decoration, whether painted or carved, must be considered from two angles: what does it represent and how is it executed. These are complementary aspects that enable us at one and the same time to capture the qualities of a man's feeling and his conception of a basic theme. Gothic iconography is extraordinarily ample: nothing is foreign to it and it embraces the whole universe. No doubt it is guided by strong theological ideas: the unrivalled drama of the Fall and the Atonement recurs again and again from the Creation to the end of time; and that great drama portrays in turn the Incarnation in the porches of the Virgin, and the Redemption in those of the Judgment, while the part played by men in the task of Salvation is represented in the porches devoted to the lives of the Saints. Everywhere links are established between the Old and the New Testaments: around Christ the Teacher, and Christ the Judge, are grouped the Precursors; around the Virgin, her ancestors of the flesh and of the spirit; the Church and the Synagogue are complementary, and the work of men leads up to their Resurrection. So that everything is presented in the form of the great doctrinal truths with which the unfolding of human history is stamped, by which it is unified. This teaching, whose principal features are necessarily constant, does, however, vary in the details of its development, and every cathedral has its own particular theme within which original lines of thought are expressed.

As striking as the doctrinal strictness is the human quality of all these figurations and the interest taken in the life of nature and the world. It is far from the gesturing humanity of the Romanesque age, haunted by terrifying visions: the flowers of the fields and the day-to-day happenings of men's lives appear everywhere. The stars preside not only over the Last Judgment but over the work of the Months, in those calendars which recall in everyday terms the slow and regular rhythm of the days. Daily life is presented there along with the incidents of trade, the social hierarchy, the moral life of men, their vices and virtues, and the achievements of scientists and philosophers: Aristotle and Pythagoras are set side by side with the old men of the Apocalypse and the choruses of angels. Gothic iconography offers to the eye an encyclopedia as well as a theological Summa, but it tends less to reproduce pedantically the Speculum Majus of Vincent de Beauvais, than freely to import its content, creating the feeling that all is engaged in this perspective of salvation—the material, vegetable and animal world as well as the diversity of men—and that the same destiny sways the whole universe. This taste for life, this raising of the curtain on the youth of the world, is one of the dominating ideas of Gothic sensibility and transforms the significance of the most majestic scenes: the Coronation of the Virgin is filled with filial piety, the Christ teaching or judging remains a man closely akin to mankind, and at the hour of judgment the Virgin and St John appeal to his pity; the same human appeal is found everywhere.

It is not surprising, therefore, that the very style of Gothic sculpture shows, all through its history, an ever-increasing naturalistic tendency. As early as the middle of the twelfth century, in the 'Portail Royal' of Chartres, a new inspiration asserts itself, which puts an end to the universe of Romanesque forms. The tight texture of the tympana of Moissac, of Beaulieu, or of Vézelay, the dramatic gestures of geometrically composed figures, are replaced by an airy, calm, and still composition which lifts its whole great mass into the freedom and space of the outside world. One should not be deceived by the ornamental pleating of the surfaces: the novelty of this art lies in its bold use of full-scale relief, in its discovery of the intrinsic monumentality of living forms, or at least in the way in which its voluminous figures placed in quietly immobile attitudes achieve conformity with the requirements of architectural décor. The pillar-statues, detached from the inner surface of the jambs, create by virtue of their projection as much as through their height and their limited gestures a vertical outline which is more emphatic than that of the engaged columns at their sides; they thus illustrate the two major principles of the new art (Plate 17).

The 'Portail Royal' of Chartres was indeed the result of many experiments which extend to Toulouse, to the Meuse, and the Poitou, and whose origins go back further than the work at St Denis; but the particular rigidity of its style, the elegant spareness of its relief, as much as the size and nobility of the tympana, make it an exemplary work, which crystallized the tendencies of the time. The sculptures as a whole are in other respects far from presenting a perfect unity of execution: these portals were originally intended to occupy a different position, set back in relation to the towers and in the shelter of a deep porch; at least five years of work had been carried out on them when, in about 1150, it was decided to bring them forward in line with the west front and to develop their embellishment. Many joins are apparent in the lateral doors, where extra lintels seem also to have been added, and the column-statues themselves are divided by date and style into three distinct groups. The oldest situated in the left-hand embrasure of the left porch (Plate 14) differs appreciably from the figures of the central porch in which the art of Chartres of 1150–1155 is clearby discernible, with its more natural folds and the fully developed beauty of the facial modelling. The narrative frieze of the capitals, the carved columns, the little superimposed reliefs on the casings of doors, introduce varied accents which recall numerous sources. But the majesty of the Christ of the central porch (Plates 23 and 24) firmly establishes the new vigorous image of man.

Bourges takes up in a strongly Burgundian style and with forms that are richer, sturdier but less detached from the mass of the building (Plate 177), the same themes and the same type of statue. And soon after, at Notre-Dame de Paris, a new stage is reached.

In the 'Porch of Saint Anne' (Plate 6) appear on either side of the majestic, effigy-like Virgin, the life-like figures of the founders of the cathedral: the bishop Maurice de Sully (Plate 4) and King Louis VII. On the top lintel, the only one dating, except for its extension pieces, from the twelfth century, the narration of the Childhood of Christ differs from that of Chartres (Plate 21), and introduces a pleasant picturesqueness. The modelling is more rounded, more solid than at Chartres, and the bodies, moulded in softer draperies, take on a more discernible form. This more fluid modelling foreshadows fundamental changes, of which the portal of Senlis (Plate 158) is one of the most striking examples. The sense of movement in the composition and the figures is just as important here as the theme of the Triumph of the Virgin, which, incidentally, came from Cambrai; it gives the impression of gold or stucco work; of a style developed for the handling of malleable substances, and here achieving monumental dignity in stone. At Sens (Plate 69), on the other hand, some twenty years later, a firmer and smoother style emerges, which was to become quite influential in the early years of the thirteenth century: at Chartres, some of the statues of the side porches of the south façade (Plate 31) recall the attenuated drapery folds and the long thin hands of the St Stephen of Sens, while at Strasbourg the workshop responsible for the sculpture of the south transept (Plates 186 and 188) would seem to offer a rather mannerized version of the same distinctive style.

Thus we come to the great sculptured ensembles of the first half of the thirteenth century, to those of Chartres, Paris, Amiens and Rheims, which demonstrate the fertility and abundance, of ideas shown (in sculpture as well as in architecture) by this classical age of French Gothic. In this field again it is Chartres which inaugurates the century. The two façades of the transepts show such decorative unity that it is indeed difficult to realize that they were not thought out during one and the same burst of inspiration, but that a succession of groups of craftsmen worked on them for nearly fifty years.

It has now been proved that when work started around the year 1200 only one porch had been planned for the north façade. Ten years later work was started on the south façade, beginning with the centre porch, or 'Porch of the Last Judgment', then the two lateral doorways—of the Martyrs, and of the Confessors. Only after 1220 was it decided to add two more porches on the north side and porticos in front of both façades; another thirty years were to elapse before the whole of this vast programme was carried out.

With its six porches in the transepts and the three still older doors of the west front, Chartres presents an exceptionally rich iconography: certain themes, such as the story of Job or of the Judgment of Solomon, until then of secondary importance, come to occupy the tympana; the meaning of this multitude of symbolic prefigurations of Christ and of the Church, drawn from the stories of the Old Testament, has recently been deciphered in an enlightening work on the sculptural programmes of Chartres Cathedral.

From the stylistic point of view, the spreading-out of works over a long period makes it possible to discern a complex evolution, in which we are now able to identify the contributors and the origins of different masters. In the sculpture of the two central tympana, those of the Coronation of the Virgin and of the Last Judgment, the simultaneous influence of Laon and Senlis is recognizable. The theme and the whole composition of the tympanum of the Virgin are directly borrowed from the west porch of Senlis. But the work of the Chartres masters has none of the vehemence of the Senlis tympanum: theirs is a much quieter style and the suppleness of the draperies, the stress laid on the solidity and roundness of the bodies, are accompanied by a particular sense of harmony, by a taste for easy gestures and attitudes which can be traced back to one of the series of carvings on the west façade of Laon. It is in that late twelfth-century style that the new sculpture of Chartres starts on its course. Until after 1220, the statues on the jamb columns seem suspended in mid-air: the feet are given hardly any support, they do not carry the weight of the body, and although the reliefs are firmer and gradually stand out further from the exceedingly narrow columns, the stress is not yet on firm definition of living forms. Some evolution in the type of the faces is apparent: hollow-cheeked and very elongated in the north porch, they become markedly firmer in the 'Porch of the Last Judgment' (Plate 33) and achieve full reality in the side porches of the south façade.

From the beginning, an effort to depict individual types of humanity can be recognized at Chartres: the St John the Baptist (Plate 46) or the David (Plate 43) of the north porch are very remarkable in this respect and herald groups like those of the 'Porch of the Confessors' (Plate 38), where the contrast between different personalities is expressed more easily and more naturally.

From approximately 1225 on, the bodies acquire a poise which until then they lacked, and rest firmly on their plinths. This can best be seen in the statuary of the detached porticos of the north façade and in the later statues of the south porches—those of St Theodore, St George, St Avitus, and St Laumer. It was at this time, too, that the workshops developed their individuality. To realize this it is only necessary to compare the statues of the two side porches of the north transept: in the right-hand one (Plate 42) the bodies are heavier, the faces have a more lively expression; here is a strong, almost restless, even troubled, art. That same feeling seems to recur in the St George of the south porch (Plate 32), whereas the complementary St Theodore is perfectly serene. In the same way, in the north portico, the very refined type represented by the St Modesta or by the Bathsheba is in sharp contrast to the heavy, round face of the Judith in the portal of Job. In some respects, however, there is consistency throughout: the supple, finely modelled draperies which flow round the figures like a clear, pale light, and perhaps even more, a certain human quality present in all the products of Chartres art which has a compelling, almost a pathetic charm. But Gothic sculpture is open to very different interpretations, and Chartres represents only one group of tendencies.

By a parallel development, starting in 1210, an art had sprung up in Paris that was fascinated by size and stability, one of its main concerns being to give to sculptured blocks a firm cohesion of surfaces. The huge scale of the resulting portals meant that they had to be strongly framed; and indeed it is by its architecture of composition, its calm and solemn volumes, that the art of Notre-Dame de Paris first impresses the spectator. The 'Porch of the Virgin' has an especial majesty; and it required an uncommon sense of composition of volumes to dare to divide the horizontality of the lintel into six great vertical figures, and to realize that this division would afford a firmer setting for the entirety of the tympanum. In the central porch one observes a similar daring: the two inner recessed orders of the arch are occupied by half-length figures of angels set perpendicularly on the curve of the arch, in such a way that one has the impression that they are radiating out from the tympanum, and that a new link has been formed between the recessed orders and the central scene. These bold experiments with the movement of volumes are the sign of a very great master. They are accompanied by a special manner of carving the stone—by a use of relief to flatten out the folds of the draperies, a technique of semi-relief in the tympana and the employment of flat stretches of medallions in bas-relief, on the stylobates of the porches, which are reminiscent of a motif that had already been adumbrated at Senlis and Sens.

The 'Porch of the Last Judgment' is plainly the work of several hands; it is even a summation of the sequence of diverse styles of the Paris workshops in the first thirty-five years of the thirteenth century. At the base, the medallions of the Virtues and Vices (Plate 9), the earliest work on the façade of Notre-Dame, executed before the 'Porch of the Virgin', have a flowing mobility which is not entirely due to the restorations of the eighteenth century, and which emanated from Sens. After an interval, the tympanum and the recessed orders of the archivolts were continued by the team which had just completed the 'Porch of the Virgin', in a similar but less austere style, as is evident in the scenes of Hell (Plate 5), which abound in a picturesque and unexpected liveliness. The last and most momentous of these changes appears in the upper tier of the central tympanum (Plate 3), where the figures of Christ in Judgment and of the angel, who on his right holds the lance and nails, reveal a completely new style: dramatic sweeps of heavy drapery creating contrasts of light and shade, and a new concept of physical beauty, supple in stance and livened in feature by the shadow of an inner wit and spirituality. This is the style which for long was considered the invention of the Rheims masters of the 'forties, but which visibly sprang to life in Paris no later than the mid-'thirties. In quite a different idiom, the lower lintel of the 'Porch of St Anne', more narrative and intimate, is evidence of another new evolution. It is clear that in Paris, as elsewhere, there was a diversity of inspiration; but what dominates the whole work is the classicism of the 'twenties, together with a sense of the need for harmony between the sculptural possibilities of the stone and those of the living form.

In this respect, as in many others, Paris is closely akin to Amiens. At Amiens, however, the arrangement of the decoration is inspired by a quite different spirit: it makes the porticos stand out from the surface of the façade; it employs effects of depth and ornamental richness; the sculptural decoration forms a continuous belt over the buttresses; statues and medallions flow in an uninterrupted series from one porch to another. And all this is in harmony with the architecture, for the whole façade is conceived of as a rich material stretched upon four vertical supports. The statues, on the other hand, have the calm, weightiness, and simplicity of surface that are the glory of Parisian sculpture. If Notre-Dame de Paris had not lost its statues, the resemblance would certainly be still more striking: even as it is, one cannot fail to be struck by the exact similarity of certain heads (Plates 3 and 115); and the draperies of the Virgin of the Visitation strongly remind one of the angels of the left porch at Paris. This solidity is further accentuated in the figures of the Magi and in that of the old man Simeon, which are grooved with strong vertical flutings. The Apostles and Prophets at the central door emphasize the massive form of the block while breaking it up with deep shadows; and the statues on the middle piers retain in their salient features the squared-off sections of the 'rough shaping' of the stone from which they were cut. The 'Beau Dieu d'Amiens' (Plate 111) combines with this solidity of volume and surface a sharpness of incision which outdoes the Parisian style of the 'twenties even at its most austere. One is therefore somewhat surprised by the contrast of style offered by the tympana at Amiens (Plates 110 and 112): here the relief is rich, almost florid, the zones of carving are crowded with narrative scenes strong in pictorial effects, and the whole surface is fragmented by the great number of small-scale figures carved in full relief. Despite their linear limitation, the small scenes which are enclosed within the medallions on the stylobate (Plates 116–124) are conceived in a more monumental spirit.

Yet all this diversity is nothing in comparison with that of the sculpture of Rheims; for if ever a cathedral has embodied all the aspects of Gothic naturalism, and all the multitude of its boldest and most contradictory experiments, it is that of Rheims. From its capitals, with their successive styles of foliage to the draped arrases used instead of medallions on the stylobates, everything affords material for research into the texture and natural movement of forms. At Rheims the façade was the subject of three distinct architectural projects. The first and second produced a 'Porch of the Last Judgment' and a 'Porch of the Saints', eventually used at the end of the north transept (Plate 88), and also many elements for a 'Porch of the Virgin', the statues of which are now found on the jambs of the doorway on the right of the west façade. It was not until 1230 that the present façade was thought of, with its porches without tympana and its sculptures housed in the points of the gables; and although the execution of the large-scale figures required by that new programme was put in hand with little delay, it was only in the mid-'fifties that the construction of the façade was actually started.

CARROLVS

The oldest statues, those in the embrasure of the right porch of the façade (Plate 59) date from about 1220. They closely resemble products of the Chartres workshops of ten years or so earlier (Plates 44 and 47): they have the same long countenances with prominent cheek-bones, the same straight, strong noses, the same treatment of beards and hair. But already some of the figures were characterized by a style of antique drapery which was doubtless due to the influence of the great Mosan goldsmith Nicholas of Verdun and which was to have a most remarkable future at Rheims. It is found again in the statues of Apostles of the 'Porch of the Last Judgment', in the statue of Christ which decorates one of the buttresses of the chevet (Plate 58), and with a completely different inflection, which certainly reveals the arrival of a new artistic personality, in the statues of the so-called 'Porch of St Sixtus' (Plate 92), in the centre of the north façade. The angel who accompanies St Remigius suggests an artist more skilled and experienced in metalwork than in stone carving, a new recruit to that 'workshop of the antique figures' who may very likely have gone on, a few years later, to produce some of the most commanding figures in the antique style. In the recessed orders and tympanum of the 'Porch of the Last Judgment' it is possible to study the subsequent development of a gentler and more melting style, which, despite its youthful charm (Plate 94) is not free from a kind of softness that is sometimes disconcerting. This relaxation of forms is accompanied by an extraordinary narrative vitality and by a multiplicity of superimposed friezes within the tympana (Plate 88). But the angels in the chevet (Plate 57), who are brothers to those of the 'Porch of the Last Judgment' (Plate 97), have greater firmness and are already akin to one of the angels on the west front (Plate 80), a statue which is commonly attributed to the last period of the 'workshop of the antique figures'. There is also a certain resemblance of effect between the draperies of the group of the Chosen (Plate 94) and those of the Virgin of the Visitation (Plate 63): a sequence of experiments seems to link together a number of very diverse works.

Around the years 1236–1240, however, soon after Jean le Loup had laid down the definitive plans for the façade, a profound transformation occurred: a master either from Amiens or from Paris introduced to Rheims the calm and simple style found in the two Virgins—of the Annunciation (Plate 67) and the Presentation in the Temple (plate 71); and the overwhelming impact of an even more recent Parisian style, that of the Christ in Judgment of the central door of Notre-Dame (Plate 3), was responsible for the crystallization of the final style of Rheims sculpture—the style of the smiling angels (Plates 67 and 81), of the Woman attendant upon the Virgin (Plate 72), of St Joseph (Plate 74) and St Nicasius (Plate 76). This does not mean that one cannot distinguish between the handiwork of various sculptors: St John (Plate 79) or the Pontiff with his hand raised in blessing in the right-hand porch (Plate 61) cannot, for example, be attributed to the sculptor who created St Nicasius; the reliefs of the faces and the flow of the draperies are evidence of quite different methods of handling the chisel, and of quite different sensibilities. Nevertheless, the whole body of this sculpture has a strong stylistic coherence: the amplitude of the surfaces, the massiveness of the figures, together with the breadth of treatment of the oblique draperies, combine with the mobility of the attitudes and the witty subtlety of the faces to produce an extremely delicate balance, in which the sculptor's keen feeling for life yields to the requirements of architectural laws.

Standing out amidst this body of work are a few figures in a quite different style, such as the group of the Visitation (Plates 63 *et seq.*) or the Prophet on the left jamb of the great central porch: in these works the inspiration of antiquity is so obvious that we must attribute them to one of the masters of the previous generation. But the works of this great artist also have the ease of attitude characteristic of the products of the new school; and his treatment of draperies reveals astonishing subtleties, almost Baroque in their lavishness of relief (Plate 64). This was the culmination of a style that was never to be recaptured, unless perhaps at Bamberg. Meanwhile Rheims was beginning to produce a multitude of works in the new style, freer, more picturesque, and more alluring than ever: the caryatids beneath the pedestals; the recessed orders of the arches (Plates 83–85); the reliefs on the casings of the doors (Plate 86); and, finally, the decorations on the reverse of the façade (Plates 105–108). Passing from antique majesty to the most spontaneous mirth imaginable, Rheims explored—in two remarkably extensive cycles, one before and the other after 1235—the whole field that had been opened up to sculptors by the broad stream of naturalistic inspiration along which the century was being carried.

In other places besides Rheims a similar evolution was taking place: in Paris, where the new style had initiated, the next stages were marked by the statues of the Apostles in the Sainte Chapelle and soon after by the delicate sculpture of the transept porches of Notre-Dame. The Virgin of the porch which opens on the rue du Cloître, on the north side of Notre-Dame (Plate 10), demonstrates the basic affinity, in spite of differences in emphasis, between the workshops of Paris and of Rheims in the mid-thirteenth century. But these two centres were not identical in inspiration: one has only to look at the Virgin of Notre-Dame and the female figure from the Presentation group at Rheims (Plate 72) to be aware of the similarity of stance and the difference in the interpretation of the human type. The grave elegance of the Paris work, as opposed to the smiling sweetness of the Rheims figure, invests the former with an aristocratic dignity and already reflects that courtly art which was to exercise so great an influence at the end of the thirteenth century and throughout the fourteenth. But the long oblique fall of the folds, the stature and supple attitude of the figures are common to both Paris and Rheims, and it is not difficult to understand why this new style, which captured such gracious charm, had so wide an influence. From 1250 onward, all French sculpture was inspired by this easy and refined naturalism: the solid, strong works of the beginning of the century were succeeded by a phase of Praxiteleanism. The tympanum surmounting the Virgin of the north porch of Notre-Dame (Plate 10), while it partakes of the same spirit, is nonetheless somewhat apart in its handling of surfaces, probably drawing upon the art of the Paris ivory carvers. Its intent is essentially narrative, and the place of honour, above the Childhood of Christ, is occupied by the Legend of Theophilus, the most celebrated of the 'Miracles of Our Lady': thus the influence of the court was reinforced by that of the theatre.

On the other hand, the 'Vierge dorée' of Amiens (Plate 129) is a direct offshoot of the art of Rheims: it was thence that it obtained its smile, its flowery richness, and its heavy stuffs hanging in deep folds. The statues on the jambs are of no great consequence; but the lintel with the group of the Apostles combines robustness with the elegance of its figures, and is one of the masterpieces of the 'fifties. A little later, the central portal at Bourges was another reflection of the same development. Here the mirth had become somewhat excessive and stereotyped (Plate 172); but it is in harmony with the delicate modelling of the tympanum, which invites the play of light, whilst the flowered recessed orders of the arches (Plate 174) are very reminiscent of those of Rheims (Plate 69). It is still around Rheims, therefore, that the art of the second half of the century pivots: even the group of the Foolish Virgins on the west front of Strasbourg (Plate 183) belongs to that line of descent.

The later evolution of Gothic sculpture hardly comes within the scope of this volume. Only the façade at Rouen (Plate 136) enables us to see, in delightful juxtaposition, the somewhat dry preciousness of the fourteenth century and the more vigorously picturesque qualities of the sculpture of the beginning of the sixteenth. A close alliance was maintained between the treatment of architecture and that of sculpture; but architecture was no longer the dominant partner: it seems more and more to have been reduced to a plastic art, and from this time onwards it was architecture that conformed to the tonality of sculpture. And it is at Rheims, once again, that we first observe the phenomenon, a little after 1250, of this reversal of the relationship between the two major techniques of craftsmanship in stone. That great façade at Rheims, which is as rich as goldsmiths' work and all covered with reliefs and sculptured motifs, is better described in terms of relief than of structure or volume; in its very conception as much as in the style of its statuary, it opened the way for all the later developments of Gothic.

This is why we may use Rheims—or, more exactly, this particular façade of it, which is so different from the original parts of the same building—to conclude our account of that first Gothic age which evolved from strict monumental discipline towards a naturalism that became increasingly flexible and pervasive. That feeling for life which had first of all penetrated the formal outlines of iconography, ended by invading even architecture and subordinating this art to its own purposes. Many commentators have noticed the parallel between the stylistic evolutions of Gothic and of Greek sculpture. Without attaching too strict an importance to such cyclical rhythms and repetitions of history, one must certainly recognize them: it appears that similar developments of the spirit, grappling with similar techniques of expression, are liable to pass through the same phases; and that the workshop of the 'antique figures' afforded the decisive and fugitive moment at which a direct contact with the classical past could sustain the researches of the great Gothic masters.

Thus it is that the sculpture of the cathedrals of the Ile de France offers, no less than their architecture, a history which it is fascinating to trace out in the details both of its inspiration and of its style. It reveals to us, together with the spatial experiments of architecture, the linked series of its meditations on mankind, on nature, on the complicities of light and modelling in relief, and on the contradictory demands of stone and likeness to life. The entirety of the works bequeathed to us by these 150 years of Gothic art is impressive no less for its love of humanity than for the vigour of its architecture; and these two things, again, are only two aspects of an art that was much more rich than either of them and disposed of many other means of expression.

JEAN BONY

All the photographs in this book were taken by Dr Martin Hürlimann,
with the exception of those used for plates 181 and 189, which were
kindly provided by Mr and Mrs Theodor Seeger, Zurich.

32

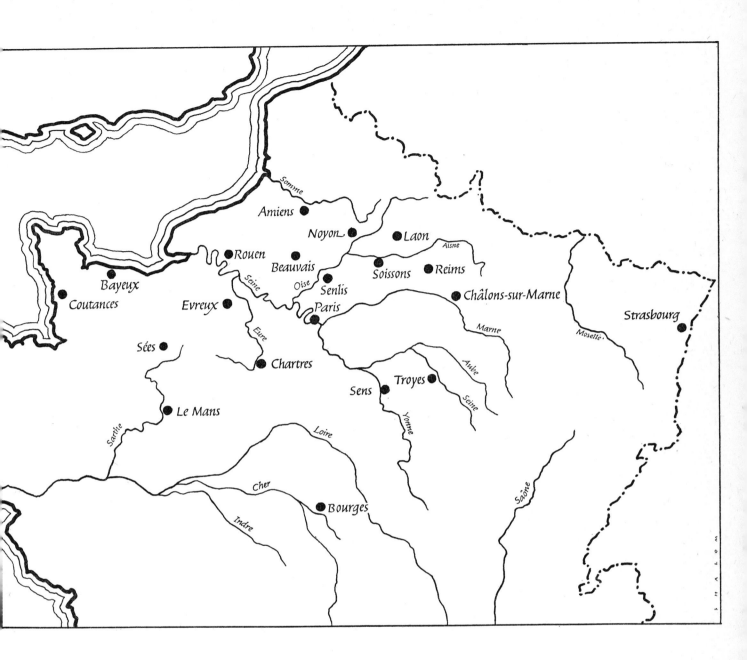

NORTHERN FRANCE SHOWING LOCATION OF CATHEDRALS

THE PLATES

THE foundation stone was laid in 1163 under Maurice de Sully who was bishop from 1160 to 1196. The choir was completed in 1182, when the High Altar was consecrated; immediately afterwards the nave was begun. The west front and twin towers were built some time between 1200 and 1250. The façades of the transepts to the north and south of the church have been renovated since 1250. Between 1235 and 1330, chapels were built between the buttresses on the north and south sides of the church and around the choir. The addition of these chapels makes the church, which consists of a nave with a double aisle on either side, appear to have triple aisles.

Notre-Dame is the last of a group of Early Gothic cathedrals, which, taking their example from the abbey of St Denis, have galleries above the inner aisles; unlike later cathedrals which were modelled upon Chartres. Nevertheless, the simple grandeur of the façade of Notre-Dame, its reliefs and ornamental detail, have been widely copied.

Colour Plate IV (p. 43). Notre-Dame, Paris, from the south-east.

1

The west front. Notre-Dame, like all French cathedrals, did not originally stand in isolation, but was set among houses. The façade was begun about 1200 and the porches were being built by 1208. Above these is the 'Galerie des Rois', containing the statues of the royal forbears of Christ. The originals were destroyed in 1793 during the Revolution, and the present statues are nineteenth-century copies.

The tier above, in the centre of which is the rose window, dates from the years 1220–1225. In 1250, the arcaded screen and the towers were built. The towers were originally intended to exceed their existing height of 226 feet.

2

View from the south, showing the south transept, which was renovated from 1258 onwards by Maître Jean de Chelles and his successors. On the right is the apse. The flying buttresses, a work of daring technical skill, were added in the late thirteenth century. In c. 1220 the cornice was raised and the roof was made steeper. The chapels with pointed gables surrounding the apse at ground level were built on between 1296 and 1330. To the left are the sacristy (modern) and the transept. The flying-buttresses of the nave were extensively restored by Viollet-le-Duc. In the foreground is the left branch of the Seine.

3

The west front, central porch. The tympanum represents the Last Judgment, c. 1225–1230. Above, Christ enthroned showing his wounds, between two angels with the instruments of the Passion. On the left is the kneeling Virgin, on the right St John as intercessor.

4

Detail from the tympanum of the 'Porch of St Anne' (Plate 6): Bishop Maurice de Sully.

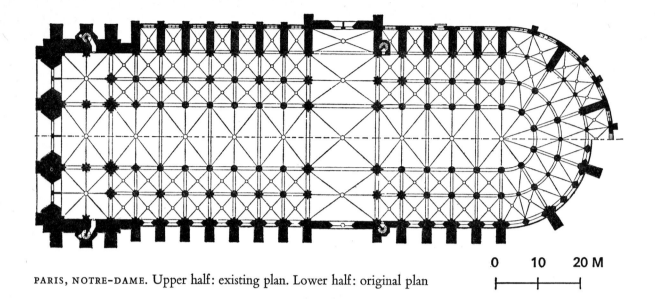

PARIS, NOTRE-DAME. Upper half: existing plan. Lower half: original plan

0   10   20 M

5

The archivolt of the tympanum. From the bottom upwards: scenes in Hell; the Chosen (patriarchs, prophets, confessors, Fathers, martyrs—distinguished by their palms—and virgins).

6

The 'Porch of St Anne', the right-hand porch of the west front. The large sculpture of the tympanum and the lintel immediately below it date from 1165–1170; they were intended for a smaller porch with a less pointed arch, and were adapted to the present porch with the help of additional decorations. The lower lintel dates from the thirteenth century (c. 1230) and represents: left, the Betrothal and the Marriage of the Virgin; right, scenes from the life of her parents, St Joachim and St Anne. The frieze of the upper lintel represents, from left to right: a prophet, the Annunciation, the Visitation, the Nativity, the Annunciation to the Shepherds, Herod and the Magi. In the tympanum is the Virgin with the Child, with hand raised in blessing, between two censing angels, with, left, Bishop Maurice de Sully and a scribe, and right, King Louis VII kneeling with a scroll.

7

The 'Porch of the Virgin', the left porch of the west front, c. 1210–1220. The statuary below in the recessed jambs is new. The beautiful ironwork of the doors is original. The lintel immediately above the doorway represents: left, three prophets; right, three kings of Judea. The frieze of the upper lintel represents the Assumption of the Virgin, with Christ, two angels, and the twelve Apostles. The sculpture in the tympanum represents the Coronation of the Virgin. The mouldings of the archivolt, from inside to outside, are made up of angels, prophets, kings, and patriarchs.

8

The 'Porte Rouge' on the north side of the choir, 1260–1270. The tympanum shows the Coronation of the Virgin with the benefactor Louis IX (canonized in 1297) and his wife; the archivolt is decorated with scenes from the legend of St Marcellus, interspersed with a motif of wild roses.

9

Relief from the socle of the 'Porch of the Last Judgment'. In the upper tier are allegorical figures of Virtues; in the lower tier are the corresponding

40

Vices. Thus, Humility, holding a shield with a dove, is enthroned above Pride falling off a horse (see Plate 28): Prudence, holding a shield with a snake, above Folly; Justice (a salamander) above Injustice.

10

Porch of the north transept, dating from the middle of the thirteenth century. Note how the figures are less formally disposed. On the central pier below, which has a foliated capital, is the Virgin. The lower frieze of the tympanum represents, from left to right: the Nativity, the Presentation in the Temple, Herod and the Massacre of the Innocents, and the Flight into Egypt. Above it is the legend of the priest Theophilus who was corrupted by the Devil but later redeemed by the Virgin.

IV PARIS: NOTRE-DAME FROM THE SOUTH-EAST

3

4

6

7

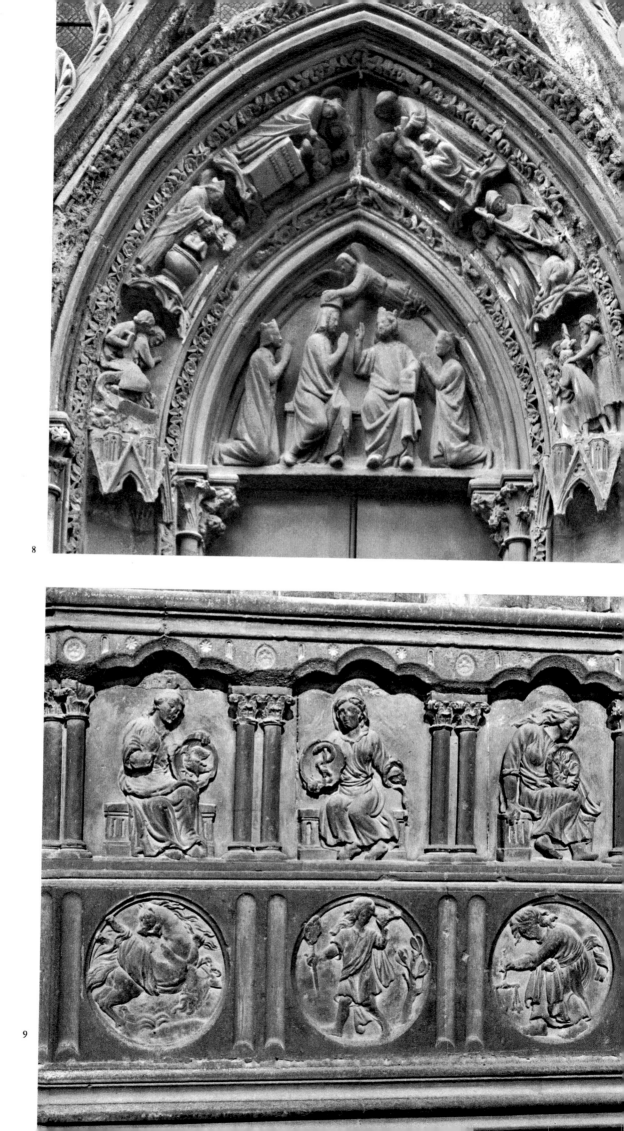

8

9

CHARTRES Plates 11–50

THE site had already been a place of worship in pagan times. The cathedral which existed in the Carolingian era has disappeared but for the central part of the crypt, the 'Caveau de Saint Lubin'. A new church, with an ambulatory and three chapels about the choir, was begun under Bishop Fulbert after fire had destroyed the previous structure in 1020. The plan roughly tallied with the plan of the present cathedral, but without the transept. In 1194 the church was again burned down. It was rebuilt on the existing foundations and crypt, with the addition of a transept. In 1220 the building was complete but for the façades of the transept and their porticos. Chartres Cathedral is the first example of a 'classic' cathedral which, instead of galleries above the aisles (as in Laon, Noyon, and Notre-Dame in Paris), has tall windows in the clerestory and high vaults in the aisles. This is one of the many features which first appeared in medieval form in Chartres Cathedral and were later quickly developed to become hallmarks of High Gothic. This edifice possesses an incomparable vigour of design and execution, unlike the often over-developed structures of the second half of the thirteenth century.

Colour Plate I (p. 17). Chartres Cathedral from the north-west.

Colour Plate V (p. 57). Chartres Cathedral: stained-glass window donated by the furriers of the city. It shows the patron saint of Spain, St James, whose relics were preserved in Compostela, appearing to the sleeping Charlemagne and urging him to make war on the heathen. (The next scene in the window is the conquest of Pampeluna.)
Iona.

11

The west front. The north tower, on the left, was begun in 1134. It once stood isolated from the church, for Bishop Fulbert's cathedral did not extend so far to the west. In 1145 the south (right) tower was built and a narthex added to connect the nave with the towers. The space between the towers was at first intended as an open portico, but, c. 1150, the west façade, with its three porches, was brought forward in line with the towers. These and the two lower storeys of the façade survived the fire of 1194. The central part of the façade was raised, c. 1210, to conform to the height of the newly erected nave. This addition was not completely successful. The rose window is too large for the delicate proportions of the lower windows, and it also detracts to a certain extent from the admirable effect of the south tower with its stone spire. Between 1507 and 1513 Maître Jean de Beauce gave the north tower, which had been damaged by lightning, a fantastically ornate Late Gothic spire, 377 feet high. For this reason it is now known as the 'Clocher Neuf'. The south tower, or 'Clocher Vieux', is 350 feet high, and carries a 148-foot spire.

12

The rose window (some 44 feet in diameter) overpowers the delicately proportioned windows of c. 1150. It still retains the original stained glass.

13

South-west corner of the south tower ('Clocher Vieux'), showing west side of the south transept. In the foreground is the 'Angel of the Sundial' which inspired Rilke's famous poem. The sundial, and

53

probably the wings, were added later. To the right is 'l'Ane qui vielle', a grotesque donkey playing a hurdy-gurdy.

14

The west porch ('Portail Royal'), c. 1145. Archaic figures by the 'Etampes master' on the left-hand jamb of the left doorway (cf. Plate 15). (For their equivalent on the extreme right see Plate 20). These elongated figures seem to float before the columns, and their clothing looks as if it has been drawn rather than sculpted.

15

The west porch. On the right are the left-hand jambs (c. 1150–1155) of the central doorway (Plate 16). The capitals of the free-standing columns represent scenes from the life of Christ and of the Virgin. On the left is the 'Doorway of the Ascension', with statues attached to the piers without pedestals, which are among the more archaic sculptures (Plate 14) at Chartres (c. 1145). In the archivolts of this doorway are representations of the Months and of the Zodiac (cf. Plate 26).

16

The west porch; left-hand jambs of the central doorway (cf. Plate 15).

17

The west porch; statues in the jambs to the right of the central doorway (c. 1150–1155). They represent figures from the Old Testament. The shorter, fuller figures are slightly more recent than the elongated ones.

18

The west porch; a prophet from the left-hand jamb of the right doorway (the 'Portal of the Virgin').

19

A king of Judea, from the left-hand jamb of the right doorway.

20

The west porch; right-hand jamb of the right doorway (cf. Plate 14). Statues carved by the 'St Denis master', c. 1145.

21

The west porch; tympanum of the 'Portal of the Virgin'. The frieze on the lower lintel represents the Annunciation, the Visitation, the Nativity, and two shepherds. On the upper lintel is the Presentation in the Temple. The relief at the top shows the Virgin enthroned, with the Child raising his hand in blessing (cf. Plate 4) between two censing angels. In the archivolt on the left are the Pisces and Gemini from the Zodiac; above are angels. (For detail on the right see Plate 25.)

22

Detail showing the shepherds at the bottom right of Plate 21. The cropping of the right-hand side of the frieze indicates that it was originally intended for a wider tympanum.

23

Central tympanum of the west porch, 'Portail Royal', c. 1150–1155. The lintel frieze represents the twelve Apostles. Above is Christ enthroned in glory, surrounded by the symbols of the four Evangelists. In the recessed arches are angels, prophets, and patriarchs.

24

Detail of the Christ in the central tympanum (Plate 23). It marks the transition from the solemnity of the Romanesque to the greater animation in Gothic sculpture.

25

Details from the right-hand side of the archivolt (Plate 15). Top: from the allegories of the Arts, 'Musica' and 'Grammatica' (with pupils and a rod). Below the former is Pythagoras as her chief representative. Below the latter is Donatus, the Roman grammarian, with writing materials.

26

Details of the 'Portal of the Ascension' (Plate 15). The Months: left, July reaping corn; right, April tending a tree; both on the left-hand side of the archivolt.

27

St Lubin administers the Extreme Unction; from an outside pillar of the south porch, c. 1230.

28

The south porch (cf. Plate 27); Pride falling off a horse.

29

The south transept from the south-west. On either side of the gable are bases for towers which

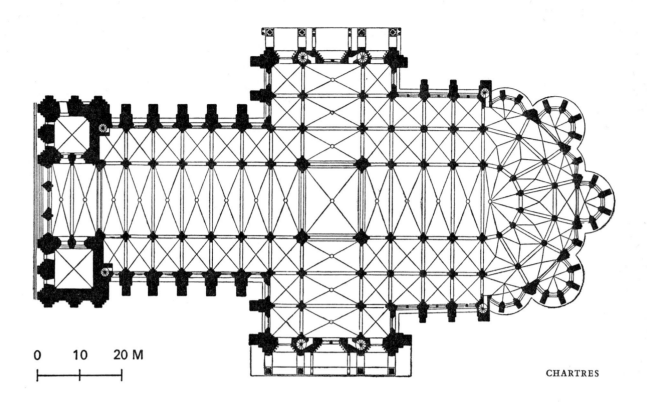

CHARTRES

were never completed. The walls are decorated with slim colonnettes. The magnificent portico was built between 1224 and 1235, after the completion of the ~~porch~~ doorways.

30

Detail from the middle doorway, central pillar: Christ, his right hand raised in blessing, his left holding the Book of Life, c. 1212–1220.

31

Details from the jambs of the left doorway of the south transept, left side. Four statues representing, from right to left: St Lawrence, St Clement, St Stephen (cf. Plate 169) and St Theodore. The rounded figure of St Theodore, with his more natural stance and his feet firmly planted on the socle, indicates that this statue is of later date than the others, having been added when the ~~portico~~ *façade* was built, c. 1215–1235.

32

Detail from the opposite jamb of the same doorway. St George in the attire of an armed knight of the thirteenth century, the counterpart of the statue of St Theodore.

33

Detail from the left-hand jamb of the central doorway of the south transept: St Paul (with the sword), St Andrew and St Peter (with the key).

34

Tympanum of the middle doorway of the south transept, c. 1212–1220, showing Christ enthroned, raising his pierced hands, between the Virgin and St John as intercessors, flanked by angels holding the instruments of the Passion. In the centre of the lintel stands the Archangel Michael with his scales; on the left (on Christ's right), the Blessed; on the right, the Dammed in Hell. The archivolt represents, left, cherubs with the Blessed; right, the Dammed with the Devil (cf. Plate 35). Above these are the hierarchies of the angels.

35

The Damned in the clutches of devils, from the recessed archivolt of the middle doorway, south portico (cf. Plate 34).

36

The left-hand jamb of the right doorway of the south portico (cf. Plate 37); St Laumer, c. 1230.

55

37

View along the inside of the portico of the south transept. In the foreground are four statues on the left jamb of the right-hand doorway. They represent, from right to left: the bishops, St Nicholas, St Ambrose, and the pope, St Leon (*c.* 1220), and, on the far left, St Laumer—a slightly more recent addition (cf. notes on Plates 31 and 32). In the background one can see the Apostles from the left jamb of the central doorway.

38

The opposite jamb of the same doorway. From left to right: St Martin, St Jerome, the pope St Gregory, *c.* 1220, and St Avitus (?), *c.* 1230.

39

St Gregory (Plate 38) with the dove of the Holy Ghost on his shoulder.

40

Portico of the north transept, begun towards 1220, as an addition to the building. Its piers consist of richly carved units which are more elaborate and less compact than those of the south portico (Plate 29). The statue on the extreme right represents St Modesta.

41

Statue on the central pier of the middle doorway of the north transept: St Anne with the Infant Virgin, *c.* 1205–1210.

42

Detail from the right doorway of the north transept, left-hand jamb: statues representing Balaam, the Queen of Sheba, and King Solomon, *c.* 1220–1225.

43

Close detail from Plate 44: King David.

44

Detail from the middle doorway of the north transept, left-hand jamb: statues representing, from left to right: Melchizedek, Abraham with Isaac bound in readiness for the sacrifice, Moses, Samuel, and King David (Plate 43), all dating from *c.* 1205–1210.

45

Close detail from Plate 44: Isaac.

46

Detail from the middle doorway of the north transept, right-hand jamb: St John the Baptist, 1205–1210.

47

Detail from the middle doorway of the north transept, right-hand jamb: St Peter.

48

Interior of the south aisle, looking east, through the transept into the ambulatory.

49

Interior of the north transept, looking east. The old pattern of main arcade (aisles), large arched galleries (vaulted) and clerestory (see Plates 159 and 164) was replaced at Chartres by a new type of elevation, in which there are only two main storeys, separated by the narrow arcading of the triforium which provides a narrow passage at the level of the lateral roofs. Since the height of the nave remained the same (121 feet at Chartres), the height of the aisles and of the clerestory windows could thereby be considerably increased. The 23-foot lancet windows and the roses above fill nearly the whole width of the bay, and continue past the springing line of the vault, which, as a result, has the appearance of floating in space. This is in direct contrast to Plate 159 in which these windows do not even start till above the springing line of the nave vaults. The piers alternate between a round core with octagonal shafts and vice-versa: a reminiscence of the system of alternating supports, which generally accompanied the use of sexpartite vaulting (see Plate 164). But at Chartres itself, the simple quadripartite type of diagonal rib-vaulting was used in preference to sexpartite, and became the rule from then on.

50

The south transept. In the centre of the rose window is Christ enthroned; in the centre lancet, the Virgin; in the side lancets, the Prophets carrying the Apostles on their shoulders.

17

21

22

24

25

26

27

28

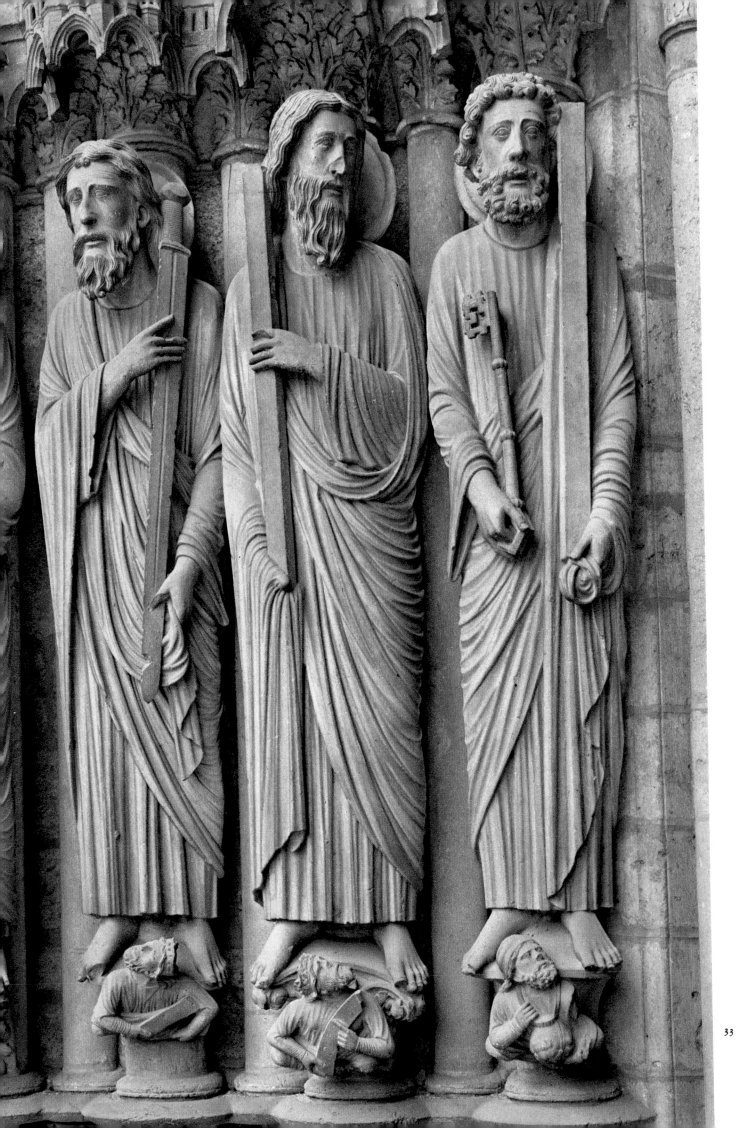

34

35

43

46

47

NOTRE-DAME de Rheims is the last of a series of churches which occupied the same site from the time when, in 496, St Remigius baptized Clovis, King of the Franks.

The present church was begun in 1211, following the destruction by fire of the preceding church in 1210; Maître Jean d'Orbais began work on the new building under Archbishop Aubri de Humbert. The choir and possibly the transept and two bays of the nave were finished in 1241. By that time, work on the statuary of the projected west porches had already been going on for at least five years. The west façade to above the rose windows, the porches, and the inner wall of the façade were built between 1254 and 1290; by 1311 only the towers remained unfinished; the north tower was completed last, in 1427.

Rheims Cathedral has for centuries been numbered among the world's masterpieces, comparable in status to the Parthenon, and, like it, the culmination of a whole era of development. Here, window tracery, which was to be such a significant feature of the later cathedrals, is encountered for the first time, though still in somewhat archaic form. In the complete harmony of its composition, Rheims surpasses its forerunner, Chartres.

As the scene of the anointing of the kings of France with the legendary Heaven-sent oil, the cathedral was closely connected with the throne. This explains the incomparable richness of the relief decoration which surrounds the main structure, and the high rank of the figures represented on the porches. In the quality of its detail, and in its worldwide architectural influence, Rheims can only be compared, yet again, with the Parthenon.

Colour Plate VI (p. 143). The large west rose window seen from the inside. In the centre is the Virgin Mary on her death-bed; round her are first twelve medallions of the Apostles, and then twenty-four medallions of angels playing musical instruments etc. The doubling of the number of tracery bars in the outer portion of the window, already a feature of Notre-Dame in Paris (see Plate 1), gave the window the same degree of luminosity throughout.

51

The west front. When the cathedral's natural setting of houses was removed towards the end of the nineteenth century, it lost its integral relationship with the surrounding town.

The lavish detail does not detract from the clarity of the design. The porches have a more dominating effect than in any other Gothic façade, while a number of features appear for the first time; for example, the windows over the doorways which replace the tympana of other cathedrals; the rose window which is placed within a pointed arch; and the incomparably delicate towers, whose stone spires, though begun, were never finished.

52–3

The gable above the central portal is decorated with a scene showing the Coronation of the Virgin, c. 1260; included are six-winged cherubs and other angels. The Virgin herself symbolizes both the Church and the 'Woman clothed with the Sun and the Moon at her feet' of the Apocalypse. Above, damage done during the First World War; below, after restoration.

54

The south tower of the west front from the south.

55

The nave from the south-east. On the left are the towers of the west front; on the right is the towerless south transept. The elaborate towers, the façade and even the sides of the cathedral are of an incomparable beauty. In the aedicules, which decorate the buttresses, are very large stone angels.

56

Buttresses with statues of angels.

57

One of the angels on the corners between the windows of the polygonal chapels of the apse (cf. Plate 58).

58

View, from the north-east, of the apse, completed in 1241. The flying buttresses were by far the most elaborate of their day, while the somewhat heavy window traceries were a new development. All the roofs are covered with lead, and the tiers of lilies on their ridges are gilded. The arcaded screens above the chapels are surmounted by 'chimaeras'.

59

Detail of the west front, showing part of the surround of the portal on the right. The statues represent St Simeon holding the Infant Jesus, St John the Baptist and Isaiah, and date from 1210–1220 (cf. Plate 44). In the left foreground are the figures of King Solomon and a bishop (cf. Plate 62).

60

Left jamb of the right portal of the west front. Two Apostles, c. 1240–1245.

61

A pope (St Sixtus?) from the left-hand portion of the surround of the same portal.

62

A bishop on one of the corners of the buttress to the right of the main portal (cf. Plate 59).

63

The Visitation (the Virgin and St Elizabeth), from the portion of the surround immediately on the right of the central porch. These approximate more closely than any other medieval figures to Greek sculpture, and upon them were modelled the statues of the Virgin and of Elizabeth which adorn Bamberg Cathedral in southern Germany.

64

Again from the right jamb of the central porch. On the left, the Annunciation; on the right, the Visitation (cf. Plates 63 and 65–68).

65

Detail of the head of the Virgin of the Visitation, shown in Plate 64.

66

St Elizabeth, mother of St John the Baptist, from the Visitation (Plate 64).

67

Detail from Plate 64: the Annunciation. The angel originally belonged to the group of St Nicasius, and is a counterpart of the figure shown in Plates 81 and 82. The angel in Plate 80 was originally meant to be placed here.

68

Detail of the Angel of the Annunciation, shown in Plate 67, which dates from c. 1240–1245.

69

The central porch viewed from the right. On the left-hand edge of the jamb is the statue of a prophet (cf. Plate 75) dating from c. 1236–1240. In the Presentation in the Temple (cf. Plates 70–72 and 74) the statues (c. 1240) represent, from left to right: Joseph, the Virgin Mary with the Infant Jesus, St Simeon, and Anna the Prophetess (or, more likely, a female attendant). In the right foreground are the three statues shown in Plate 59. The figures in the archivolt represent angels and ancestors of Christ.

70

Detail from Plate 69: Joseph, the Virgin Mary and St Simeon.

71

Detail from Plate 70: the Virgin Mary.

72

Detail from Plate 69: Anna the Prophetess (or an attendant).

73

A bishop on one of the corners of the buttress to the right of the left doorway of the west front.

74

Detail from Plate 70: Joseph.

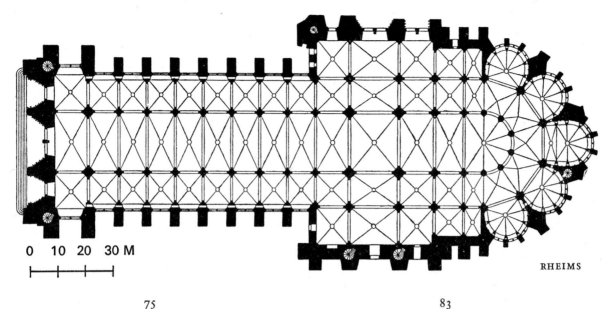

0 10 20 30 M

75

Detail from Plate 69: statue of a prophet (resembling Greek representations of Ulysses).

76

Head of the martyr, St Nicasius (cf. Plate 80).

77

A deacon and an Apostle from the right jamb of the left portal on the west front.

78

St Eutropia, the sister of St Nicasius, to the immediate right of Plate 77.

79

Young Aspostle (St John?), from the buttress to the immediate right of Plate 78.

80

Statues from the jamb of the left porch, left-hand side. They represent St Nicasius (Plate 76), and an angel which was originally meant for the Annunciation group (Plate 67). The angel represents a late form of the 'antique figure style' which had previously inspired the sculptors of the north transept doorways (Plate 92) and of the east end (Plate 57).

81

The smiling angel who stands to the right of St Nicasius (Plate 80). The Angel of the Annunciation (Plates 67 and 68) is its counterpart.

82

Detail of Plate 81. The figure is known as 'Le Sourire de Reims', and is one of the most beautiful angels in Christian art. The head was broken off by shell-fire in September 1914, and was later restored.

83

Two angels and part of the famous foliage of Rheims from the archivolt of the right-hand porch of the west front.

84

Archivolt detail from the west portal.

85

The archivolt of the left portal of the west front. The sleeping figure of Jesse can be seen at the bottom.

86

Close-up of smaller reliefs from the right portal: Virtues and Vices (?). The top figure is a cherub.

87

St Helena from the left jamb of the left portal of the west front.

88

View of the façade of the north transept—one of the oldest portions of the cathedral. Below is the porch of St Sixtus, the first Bishop of Rheims, whose statue adorns the central pier (cf. Plate 91). The statues of the jamb represent, on the left: St Nicasius holding his head in his hands, between his sister Eutropia and an angel; on the right, the figures reproduced in Plate 92. In the tympanum are reliefs depicting the legends of St Remigius and St Nicasius (cf. Plates 98 and 100). The statue in the aedicule of the buttress to the left of the rose window is shown in detail in Plate 89, those to the right in Plate 90. The tympanum of the porch on the left (the portal of the 'Beau Dieu') represents the Last Judgment.

89

Statue (before 1241) in the aedicule to the left of the rose window of the north transept (see Plate 88), representing either a royal saint or Philip II of France.

90

To the immediate right of the rose window of the north transept (see Plate 88) are statues of Eve holding a small dragon (in place of a snake) and a royal saint (possibly St Louis).

91

A statue of the pope St Callistus from the trumeau of the central portal of the north transept. This statue is generally taken to represent St Sixtus.

92

Central porch; three statues from the right-hand jamb. In the centre is St Remigius to whom a dove is bringing the vessel containing the holy unguent with which to anoint the Frankish king, Clovis, and his followers. To the left, Clovis (?); to the right, an angel, c. 1230.

93, 95

Third and fourth tiers of the tympanum of the 'Portal of the Last Judgment' (cf. Plate 88): frieze representing the Resurrection of the Dead, c. 1230.

94

The Blessed, from the left half of the second tier of the same tympanum.

96

The lowest tier of the tympanum: The Dammed being dragged by devils into the bottomless pit. Among the Dammed are a king, a bishop, a monk, and other dignitaries and plutocrats, showing that neither rank nor holy orders can prevent damnation.

97

Detail from the left half of the lowest tier of the same frieze (cf. Plate 96). The souls of the Chosen are brought by angels to 'Abraham's Bosom'. The hands of the angels are covered, as was the custom at Byzantine ceremonial functions (cf. Plate 99).

98

Detail from the tympanum over the central portal of the north transept (Plate 88); left half of the frieze immediately above the doorway, representing the beheading of St Nicasius.

99

Detail from Plate 97: two angels.

100

Detail from the second tier of the tympanum of the central doorway of the north transept (Plate 88): St Remigius as a child on his mother's knee curing Montanus of his blindness.

101

View from the south aisle through the south transept into the ambulatory.

102

Interior of the nave, looking towards the choir. It is about 45 feet wide and 128 feet high, and in elevation follows the three-tiered 'classic' design of Chartres Cathedral (Plate 49). The traceries are among the earliest to have been fully developed, and the proportions of the whole inner structure are perfect.

103

Oblique view from the north transept through the double aisle into the choir. Note the diminishing heights of the capitals.

104

One of the capitals. They are divided, horizontally, into two parts and, vertically, continue the colonnettes forming the piers. It is in Rheims Cathedral that foliage is reproduced in its natural form for the first time in Gothic architecture. Here, Joshua and Caleb are shown fighting over a basket of grapes.

105–108

Unique reliefs on the interior of the façade on either side of the main portal, c. 1260.

105. The Massacre of the Innocents (sixth tier on the left side of the main portal).

106. Joachim at the golden gate (third tier left).

107. Top (fifth tier right): angel announcing the birth of St John to St Elizabeth and to Zacharias. Centre (fourth tier): St John the Baptist with the Lamb between two disciples. Below (third tier): St John preaching repentance to Herod and Herodias. In the panels between are the famous 'leaves of Rheims'.

108. Communion of the knight (Abraham and Melchizedek [?]) (first tier right). This represents the ideal image of a crusader in the armour of the thirteenth century.

52

53

56

57

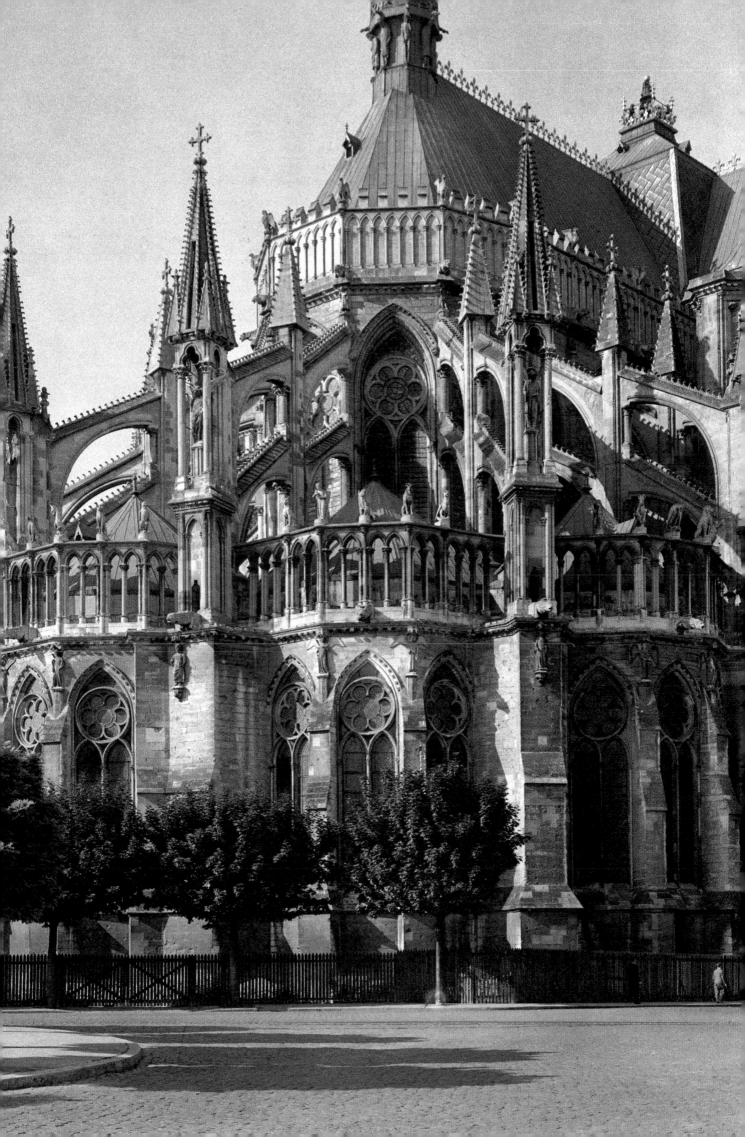

73

74

75

76

89

90

93

94

97

98

THE cathedral at Amiens (Notre-Dame) was built on the site of an earlier church, which was destroyed by fire in 1218. Maître Robert de Luzarches began the nave in 1220. The west front up to and including the rose window was finished in 1236, by which time the cathedral had already been put into service; the transept had reached the level where the triforium begins. The chapels about the choir were completed in 1247 and the upper storeys of the apse around 1270.

The choir is flanked by double aisles, and has a single ambulatory. There are only single aisles on either side of the nave. Amiens is the largest of all Gothic cathedrals, occupying an area of more than 9,000 square yards and having a capacity exceeding 260,000 cubic yards. More elegant than Chartres and Rheims, without the abstract coolness and aloofness of later buildings, it has come to be regarded as the 'classic' cathedral. Many later cathedrals, notably Tours, Cologne, Bruges, and Antwerp, have choirs similar in plan to that of Amiens. The statuary of the porches has influenced church sculpture all over Europe; it derives from that of Paris, while anticipating that of Rheims. When the Revolution threatened to destroy it, the citizens of Amiens rallied to save their cathedral.

Colour Plate VII (p. 149). The rose window of the north transept with the lancet windows of the 'claire-voie' below provide a unified, colourful mass.

109
The west front. The composition of this façade lacks the clarity of Notre-Dame in Paris and of Rheims Cathedral. The height of the relatively narrow nave meant that the rose window had to be placed too high up, above a double gallery over the porches. The façade to above the level of the rose window (subsequently modified) was completed in 1236. The top section of the south tower (right) was added after 1366 and that of the north tower between 1389 and 1410.

110
The central porch of the west front. On the pier dividing the doorway is a statue of Christ (Plate 111). In the recessed archivolt are statues of apostles and saints, and on the jambs, statues of prophets. In the tympanum are representations of the Resurrection, and of the Last Judgment 1230–1235.

111
Trumeau of the central portal: Christ standing on a lion and a basilisk, known as 'Le Beau Dieu d'Amiens'.

112
Quatrefoil decoration of the socles of the left-hand porch of the west front (cf. Plates 117 and 118).

113
The right porch ('Portal of the Virgin') with the Virgin and Child (c. 1220–1225) and, on the right, Christ and the prophet Amos in shepherd's attire.

114
Head of the Virgin on the central pier of the 'Portal of the Virgin', c. 1220–1225 (see Plate 113).

115
Detail from the Annunciation (see Plate 116).

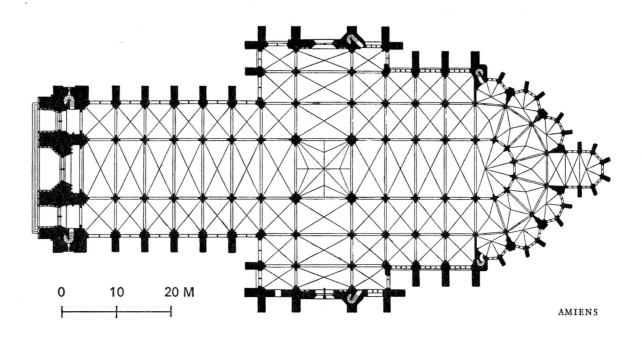

116

The right jamb of the 'Portal of the Virgin' (Plate 113). The statues represent from left to right: The Annunciation (Plate 115), the Visitation, and the Presentation in the Temple, with Simeon on the extreme right. The quatrefoils represent from top left to bottom right: Daniel facing the Rock, Gideon and the Fleece, the Message to Zacharias, the Message to Abraham, the Flight into Egypt, the Fall of the Idols in Egypt, Moses and the Burning Bush, Aaron with the Flowering Staff, the Birth of St John, the Recording of the Name of St John, Christ and the Doctors in the Temple, and the Return from Egypt.

117–118

Quatrefoils from the socles of the left porch of the west front (Plate 112). In the top tier, signs of the Zodiac; in the bottom tier, the Labours of the Months. Such reliefs are among the first in medieval art to represent details of daily life within the context of religious iconography.

119

The socle of the trumeau of the central porch (Plate 110): King David.

120

The socle of the trumeau of the 'Portal of the Virgin' (Plate 113): the Expulsion, showing Adam and Eve and the Angel with the Sword of Fire.

121–122

Quatrefoils from the socles of the 'Portal of the Virgin' (Plate 113). Above, the construction of the ship that brought the Magi and the Voyage of the Three Magi; below, Sins (?).

123

The sin of Despair.

124

The sin of Cowardice: an armed man fleeing from a hare.

125

Outside corner of the left-hand jamb of the central porch. The statues represent the prophets, Nahum, Daniel, and Ezekiel (holding a rolled scroll).

126

Tympanum of the south transept porch. The story of St Honoratus from the second frieze (see Plate 129).

127

Quatrefoil from the socle of the right-hand jamb of the left porch: the Month of March represented by a man working his vineyard, dating from *c.* 1225.

128

The Annunciation from the exterior of one of the south side chapels, fourteenth century.

129

The south transept porch, dating from *c.* 1250. The statue of the Virgin on the pier dividing the doorway is known as the 'Vierge dorée'. She is flanked on either side of the doorway by a censing angel and a group of three saints. The lintel or lower frieze of the tympanum represents the twelve apostles, conversing in pairs. Above is the frieze telling the story of the life of St Honoratus. On the right of the first tier of this frieze he is represented as the son of a poor farmer tilling the land (cf. Plate 126). The second tier shows the saint celebrating Mass, and the miraculous cures that take place at his tomb. The top tier shows his relics being carried to the church in solemn procession, with the sick hopefully kneeling before the coffin. Above this is a relief showing the Christ on the crucifix of a neighbouring church inclining his head in acknowledgement. Beside him are the Virgin Mary, St John and two angels; the innermost band of the archivolt is also decorated with angels.

130

View up the nave into the choir, the lower portion of which was completed in 1247, the upper sections towards 1270. In contrast with the older central aisle of the nave (Plate 132), these latter are typically *rayonnant* in style, with their elaborate tracery, and the triforium which has acquired the character of thin open-work. The nave is 48 feet wide and 141 feet high.

131

North aisle and part of the north transept seen from the choir.

132

The nave was built between 1220 and 1236. The piers resemble those in Rheims Cathedral, but are more slender. The triforium has a more solid appearance than the open-work triforium of the choir, which is of later date. The colonettes, continuous from floor to vault-springers, give the nave a feeling of height and unity.

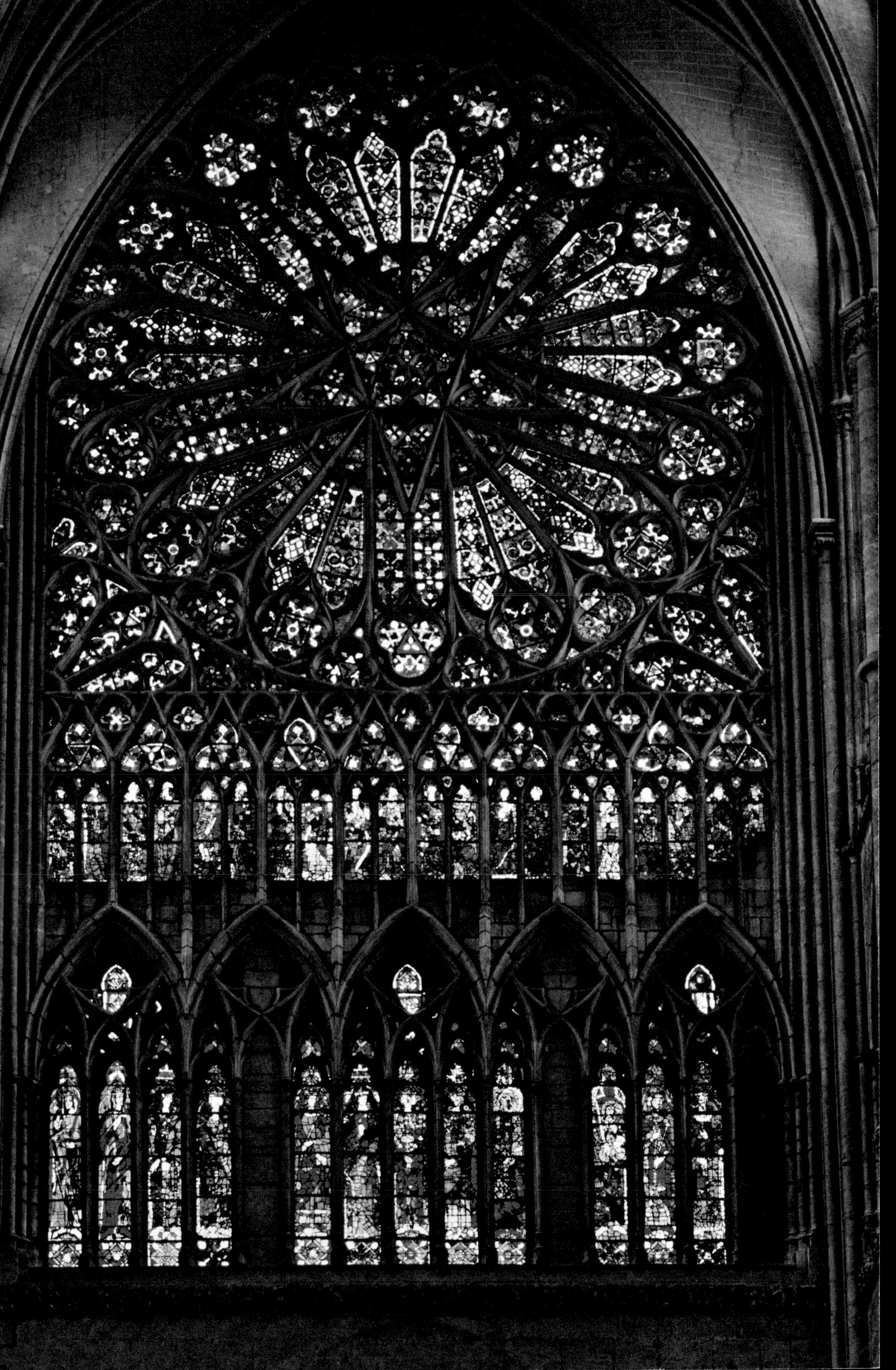

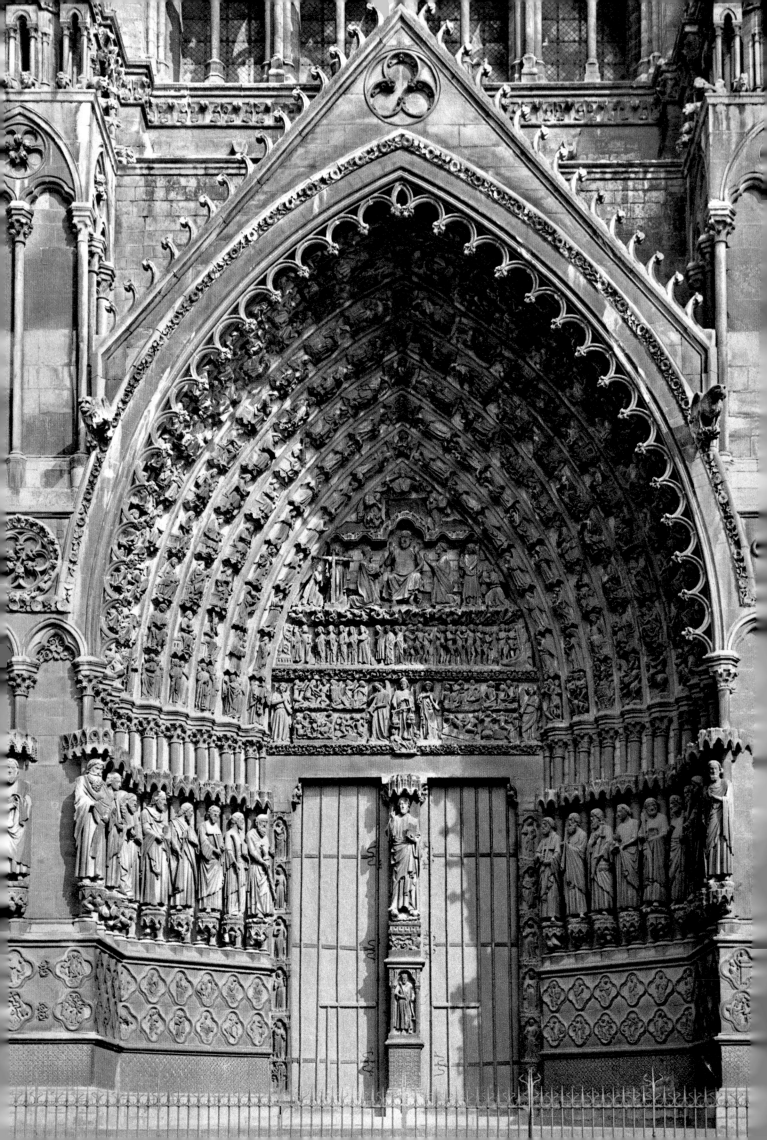

112

113

120

123

126

127

BEAUVAIS
Plates 133, 141

THE cathedral at Beauvais (St Peter) was built on the site of a tenth-century church, part of which has survived to the present day. The cathedral, a building of huge proportions, was begun in 1225, and the choir with its double aisle on either side was completed in 1272. The preponderance of open-work over solid masonry is even greater than in the reconstructed abbey of St Denis (later than 1231). The vault is the highest in Gothic architecture (about 155 feet, well over twice the average height of a modern five-storeyed office building). In 1284, the vaulting fell in. When rebuilding was begun, the piers were doubled in the choir. In 1374, when the choir was complete, work was suspended. It was not taken up again until 1500, when Maître Martin

Chambiges undertook the erection of the south transept, which was finished in 1548. The central tower collapsed in 1573. The nave was never built.

133
The cathedral from the north-east. Beauvais Cathedral suffered relatively little damage when the surrounding part of the town was destroyed in 1940. The photograph was taken in 1947.

141
The choir. In the part of the choir on the left of the picture the piers were doubled after the roof collapsed in 1284. The windows above the triforium, which also has windows, are over 52 feet high.

ROUEN
Plates 134–140

IN the cathedral at Rouen (Notre-Dame) all periods of medieval architecture are represented. When the original Romanesque cathedral was destroyed by fire in 1200, remains of it were incorporated into the façade. In 1201 rebuilding was begun under the architect Jean d'Andely; two of the west doorways date from that period. It was originally planned with galleries over the aisles of the nave, but the idea was dropped during construction. The basic structure was finished before 1250. The north and south fronts of the transept (c. 1280) are famous examples of the *style rayonnant* at its purest, as is the Lady-chapel (1302–1320) behind the choir. The blind tracery and the decoration of the gables of the west front are very early examples of the *style flamboyant* (1370–1420). The south tower, over 250 feet high, and the central

part of the west front (1509–1514) are masterpieces of the final phase of Late Gothic architecture. The tower, known as the 'Tour de Beurre', was built between 1485 and 1507. It is so called because the money for its construction came from payments for dispensations permitting the consumption of butter during Lent. It has affinities with the 'Clocher Neuf' at Chartres (Plate 11).

134
The cathedral from the south-west. The old part of the town between it and the Seine was razed to the ground during the war; since then many of the houses have been rebuilt. The photograph was taken in 1949. The 512-foot-high central spire was rebuilt in cast-iron between 1827 and 1877, after the original spire had been destroyed by lightning in

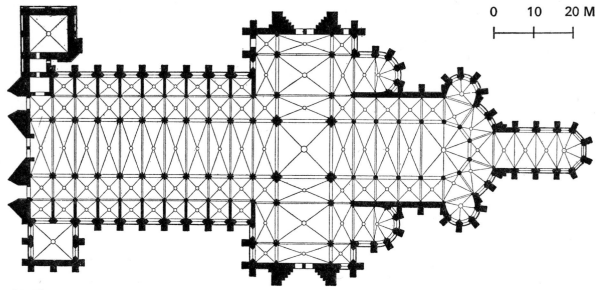

ROUEN

1822. To the left of the picture is the façade with the 'Tour St Romain' and the 'Tour de Beurre'. To the right of the choir is the Lady Chapel, 1302–1320.

135
Jamb of the north transept portal ('Portail des Libraires'): quatrefoils with fantastic mythical animals.

136
West front. The Early Gothic porches to either side of the main portal are set under round-headed arches which, in spite of appearances, are of the same date. On each side of the arch which frames the rose window, are three gables in the *style flamboyant* (1370–1420), rich in statuary. Above these, again, can be seen the earlier style window traceries and turrets. The whole central section was renovated in 1509–1514 by Jacques Roland le Roux, and is a

superb example of Late Gothic at its most ornate. The magnificent rose window, which resembled the 'flaming rose' of Evreux Cathedral was damaged, and is boarded up.

137
View of the choir and nave. The galleries in the nave were not completed (cf. Plate 139).

138
The tower above the crossing; a lantern-tower open on the inside, a typically Norman trait.

139
One of the piers of the nave, seen from the transept. Above are the openings intended for the gallery, which was never built.

140
Late Gothic staircase in the north transept.

For note on Plate 141 see Beauvais Page 171

SEES   Plates 142–143

THE cathedral at Sées (Notre-Dame) is relatively small, typically Norman, and its nave dates from *c.* 1240. The transept and the choir were built 1270–1290. The interior is in the mature *style rayonnant*.

142–143
The rose windows of the transepts seen from the interior. The lower one is based on that of Notre-Dame, Paris, shown in Plate 2.

THE cathedral of Bayeux (Notre-Dame) incorporates parts of the nave and façade of a church which had been dedicated in 1077. The nave arcades were rebuilt and decorated with diaper work, chevron and beakhead ornament in the middle of the twelfth century. The piers of the nave were adapted to the Gothic style at the beginning of the thirteenth century, together with the aisles. The choir was rebuilt c. 1230, and the clerestory of the nave in about the middle of the thirteenth century: the transept, the porches, the exterior of the façade, and the towers, shortly after. The chapels to the north and south of the aisles were added at the end of the thirteenth, and the beginning of the fourteenth century. The 262-foot-high tower above the crossing was built in the fifteenth century during the reign of Louis XI. The cathedral was allowed to fall into decay, and towards the middle of the nineteenth century it was decided to pull it down. A civil engineer named Flachat, however, saved the edifice by rebuilding the piers supporting the tower from their founda-

tions up. This was the first reconstruction of its kind.

144
The choir from the south-east; it exemplifies the style of Normandy: severe and uncompromising. Apart from the projecting east chapel, the remaining polygonal chapels have been integrated with the ambulatory by a special form of roof structure which includes a tier of pointed arches forming a parapet. The turrets which flank the apse, and the lancet windows without any tracery are also typical of the architecture of Normandy. The tower above the crossing is Late Gothic.

145
View up the nave towards the High Altar. The nave arcades are Romanesque with chevron and beakhead ornament. The clerestory and the choir are Gothic. The arches of the gallery above the choir are typically Norman in style. The small singers' gallery has been added to the balustraded wall-passage on the north side of the nave.

THE original Romanesque nave and the façade of Coutances Cathedral were rebuilt during the years following 1203, when the duchy of Normandy was united with the Crown of France. The choir was rebuilt c. 1240–1260. The double aisles derive from Bourges, but are adapted to the local style of Normandy. This cathedral, which is too little known, possesses an impressive towered façade. The towers, with their interlocked turrets, reminding one of crystal formations, and the buttresses with their little stone spires reinforce the effect of the beautifully proportioned east end.

146
South aspect, showing the tall south tower of the west front on the left. Typical of the architecture of Normandy, and, incidentally, of English Gothic architecture, are the elongated openings of the towers, the lancet windows without tracery—as, for example, in the transept—and the high tower over

the crossing. The chapels of the aisles were built later, between 1370 and 1386. The houses surrounding the cathedral were destroyed in 1944.

147
View up the interior of the nave, with light coming from the central tower (see Plate 149). The elevation of the apse recalls Le Mans, but is less elegant. A simple balustrade with tracery replaces the triforium of earlier cathedrals. The vault has a ridge rib, which shows English influence.

148
The arcade between the high inner and lower outer aisle on the north side; in the background, the beginning of the ambulatory.

149
The interior of the central tower. The opening in the centre of the vaulted roof was used for hoisting up building materials.

THE cathedral of St Julian has a Romanesque nave which was consecrated in 1158. In 1217 a new Gothic choir was begun. The relics of the saint were interred there in 1254, and in 1270 this part of the new building was finished. The south transept was added in 1387, the north transept dates from 1403—c. 1430. The general design of the choir of Le Mans Cathedral is based on that of Bourges Cathedral; its forms are akin to those of Coutances (Plate 147), though more elegant, better balanced, more truly High Gothic. There is a hint, here and there, in this masterpiece of Gothic architecture, of the regional style of Normandy.

150

The choir from the south-east. It has a double aisle on either side, and a double ambulatory. The surrounding chapels project exceptionally far. If Beauvais is the tallest of the Gothic cathedrals, Le Mans has the most highly developed system of flying buttresses, spreading their magnificent wings from the crystalline facets of the chapels. In the complicated system of buttressing about the polygon formed by the choir, double buttresses unite above the buttress piers to form single arches connecting with the apse. Here we have the principles of sound construction finding perfect aesthetic expression. To

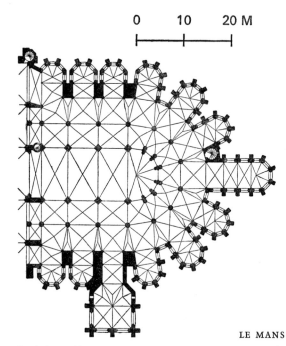

LE MANS

the left is the Late Gothic south transept, begun in 1387, with its unfinished tower.

151

The porch built on to the south side of the nave between 1150–1155, with its portico. Behind is the west wall of the south transept, with its magnificent window tracery.

EVREUX   Plates 152–153

THE cathedral of Notre-Dame d'Evreux incorporates parts of a church that was built in the early twelfth century. The choir, which is wider than the nave, was begun c. 1260 and completed towards 1310. This cathedral, in which tracery and glass fulfil the role of masonry in older architecture, has affinities with the new nave of St Denis and the choir of Amiens. The west bay of the choir was built only after 1379. The transept dates from the beginning of the fifteenth century; the central tower, from 1467; the tracery on the north façade, from 1511–1531.

152

Interior of the north transept. The rose window, one of the most striking examples of the *style flam-*

boyant, was built between 1511 and 1531. The other decorations date from the same period.

153

The apse. In most cathedrals the apse has round pillars (cf. Plates 137 and 147). In Evreux Cathedral, however, it is supported on compound piers, which has the effect of making the choir an integral part of the nave. It is a typical example of Gothic 'transmutation of masonry' into tracery and glass. Even the triforium has become a tier of windows, a device first employed in the rebuilding of the abbey of St Denis, begun in 1231. The tracery of the clerestory windows is of the *rayonnant* type; the triforium was renovated in the Late Gothic *flamboyant* style, between 1498 and 1515.

LAON Cathedral (Notre-Dame) was begun in *c.* 1165 under Bishop Gautier de Mortagne. By 1174 the choir, with semicircular apse—which included an ambulatory but had no chapels—was finished; also the east wall of the transept, which had rounded arches in the galleries. The transept and five bays of the nave (using the rounded arch) were completed between 1178 and 1190. The remaining part of the nave, the west front and the central tower above the intersection of the nave and transept, were built between 1190 and 1205. In that year the apse was demolished and the choir was extended to its present size and rectangular shape.

Laon Cathedral illustrates the full development of the type of church building with galleries above the aisles, which derived from Romanesque prototypes and became common in northern France from 1150. Notre-Dame, Paris is another example. Hardly any Gothic building has exercised such a widespread influence on European architecture, especially on Early Gothic architecture in Germany. The magnificent central tower, open on the inside like those in Normandy, was copied in Lausanne Cathedral, at Trier and at Dijon. The other towers, admired from the outset for their open, airy design, were likewise imitated at Lausanne and also at Bamberg and Naumburg. The capitals of the arcades of the galleries possess wonderful foliated ornaments, which represent a happy merger between Romanes-

que stylized design and natural treatment. They, too, were widely imitated, notably in Magdeburg Cathedral.

154

The cathedral from the south-west. Seven towers were originally planned, but only four were built. They were all meant to have spires.

161

The towers of the west front, viewed from the north-east. Even in Gothic times these were regarded as particularly beautiful. The flying buttresses were added early in the thirteenth century. Part of the tower of the north transept is to be seen on the left.

162

The tower of the south transept.

163

The south tower of the west front with the sculptured oxen.

164

The nave and transept, and the choir of 1205, with its flat end wall replacing the original apse. The nave, with its four tiers and sexpartite vaults, bears kinship with Notre-Dame de Paris. Here, however, we get an impression of greater strength and unity, which is largely due to the triforium.

NOYON   Plates 155, 159–160

THE cathedral at Noyon (Notre-Dame) was begun about 1150 on the site of an older building which dated back to Merovingian and Carolingian times. Parts of the choir were in use by 1157, though it was not finished until 1185 (four piers of the choir were renovated in 1477). The transept was built *c.* 1170, and though plans for the nave date from about this time, the western end was completed only in the thirteenth century. The nave originally had sexpartite vaults which collapsed during a fire in 1293, and were replaced by quadripartite ones. The vaulting east of the intersection of the transept and the nave collapsed a century and a half later, and was reconstructed between 1460 and 1462.

This cathedral is one of the oldest examples of Early Gothic architecture.

155

View from the south-west, showing the rounded south transept which resembles a choir. The north transept is similar, as can be seen in Plate 160, which shows the interior.

159

View up the nave towards the choir. The alternating round and compound piers were originally designed to support sexpartite vaults (cf. Plate 164). The lower arches are plain and somewhat archaic in shape. The side elevation of the nave consists of four

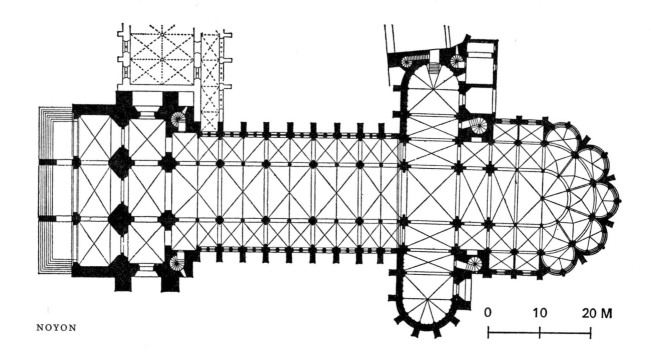

NOYON

storeys: main arcade, gallery, triforium, and clerestory (cf. Laon Cathedral, Plate 164).

160
The interior of the north transept. This transept,
like the one in Soissons (Plate 167), ends in a semi-

circle. It possesses archaic elegance. The proportion
of solid masonry to window area is astonishingly
small. Originally, the arches below the triforium
were open and contained stained glass like the others.
All the stained glass has disappeared. Note the in-
discriminate use of rounded and pointed arches.

CHALONS-SUR-MARNE   Plates 156, 165

THE cathedral of St Stephen. In a corner between
the choir and the transept are Romanesque towers,
but the choir itself was renovated in the second half
of the thirteenth century. The nave itself was built
soon after 1250. The ambulatory and the chapels
about the choir were altered c. 1300 and the vaulting
of the nave restored after a fire in 1668.

156
The cathedral from the north-west.

165
Oblique view of the interior of the nave; this is a
typical example of the *rayonnant* style. The windows
have traceries and the triforium has developed into
a series of minute windows.

SENLIS   Plates 157–158

THE cathedral of Senlis (Notre-Dame) is a building
of great charm which presents many phases of the
development of Gothic architecture. It was begun in
1153, and consecrated in 1191, though the transept
was added only c. 1240. The clerestory of the choir
and the transept fronts were burned down in 1504,
and rebuilt between 1506 and 1515.

157
View from the east, showing the upper part of the
Late Gothic choir (1506–1515). The south-west
tower is Early Gothic.

158
The west front, which has retained many Romanesque features. The Early Gothic porch (c. 1180) is

176

one of the most beautiful of its kind. It is characterized by a broad lintel over the door representing the Death and the Assumption of the Virgin. In the tympanum above is to be seen the Coronation of the Virgin. The tracery of the large central window is Late Gothic (sixteenth century).

For notes on Plates 159–160 see Noyon Page 175
For notes on Plates 161–164 see Laon Page 175
For note on Plate 165 see Châlons-sur-Marne Page 176

SOISSONS   Plates 166–167

THE cathedral of St Gervais and St Protais, often referred to as Notre-Dame, consists of two distinct parts, one Early Gothic, the other High Gothic. The Early Gothic part is divided into four storeys: arcade, gallery, triforium, and clerestory; whereas the latter, more homogeneous part has only three. The Early Gothic south transept having been completed some time during the last quarter of the twelfth century, the rest of the church was built to a new plan. The choir was consecrated in 1212, but the nave was not finished until some eighteen years later. Badly damaged in the First World War, the cathedral was afterwards substantially restored. It has served as a model for many smaller churches, particularly the choir design, where the vaulting of the surrounding chapels is integrated with that of the ambulatory, and the comparatively straightforward design of the buttresses.

166

The nave and the choir, which were begun soon after the completion of the Early Gothic transept (Plate 167). They represent a more highly developed style of Gothic, with their three storeys and tall clerestory windows which start well below the springing line of the vaults. The windows show the influence of Chartres, as do the quadripartite vaults which were largely destroyed in the First World War, but skilfully renovated.

167

The south transept, which ends in an apse like that of a choir. It is a gem of Early Gothic architecture; akin to Noyon (Plate 160), it is more elegant and more harmoniously conceived. There is a more telling use of the pointed arch here than at Noyon. On the left is a large two-storeyed chapel.

SOISSONS

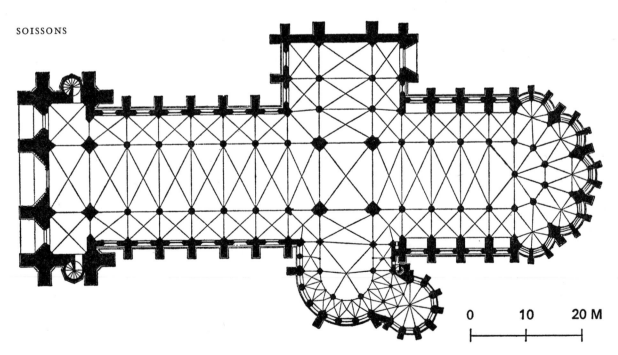

0   10   20 M

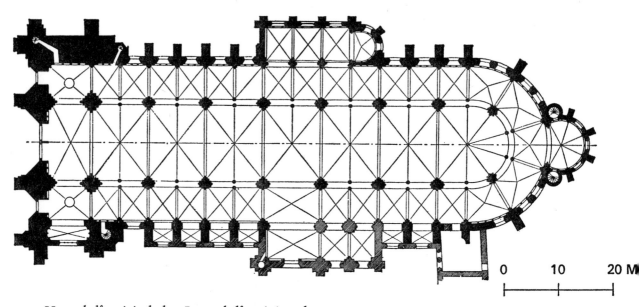

SENS. Upper half: original plan. Lower half: existing plan

SENS   Plates 168–169

THE cathedral of St Stephen was begun under Archbishop Henri Sanglier, probably *c.* 1128, but was built mostly to a new design between 1145 and 1160.

The original transept did not rise above the aisles. The present transept, which is both higher and wider, was built in the years 1490–1517. In order to give it the required width, two whole bays on either side of the church had to be knocked out.

Sens Cathedral is nearly contemporary with the abbey of St Denis, but differs from it in that it has no galleries above the aisles. The arrangement of St Denis was followed in such Early Gothic cathedrals as Noyon, Laon, and Paris. Sens Cathedral may have served as an example for cathedrals built in High Gothic style, like Chartres, Rheims, and Amiens.

The cathedral retains from its first design a number of Romanesque features: these are most apparent in the aisles, in the plain round arches of the wall arcade, and in the domed rib-vaults. The church possesses magnificent tapestries.

168

The west front. Only the porch and the lower storeys of the left-hand section remain as built between 1180 and 1200. The south tower collapsed in 1267, destroying the upper portions of the façade which was rebuilt in the thirteenth and fourteenth centuries.

169

St Stephen attired as a deacon, on the central pier of the main doorway, 1195–1210 (cf. Plate 31). The sole surviving statue of the porch.

TROYES   Plate 170

THE cathedral of St Peter and St Paul was begun as early as 1208, but the work progressed slowly. The choir was completed by 1250, but the transept was still unfinished at the end of the thirteenth century, and the nave, which had been started before 1300, was built mostly between 1450 and 1500. The

building, with its triforium broken up into a series of minor windows, is typically *rayonnant* in style (cf. Plates 130, 141, 151 and 165).

170

View up the nave towards the choir.

133 BEAUVAIS

134—140 ROUEN

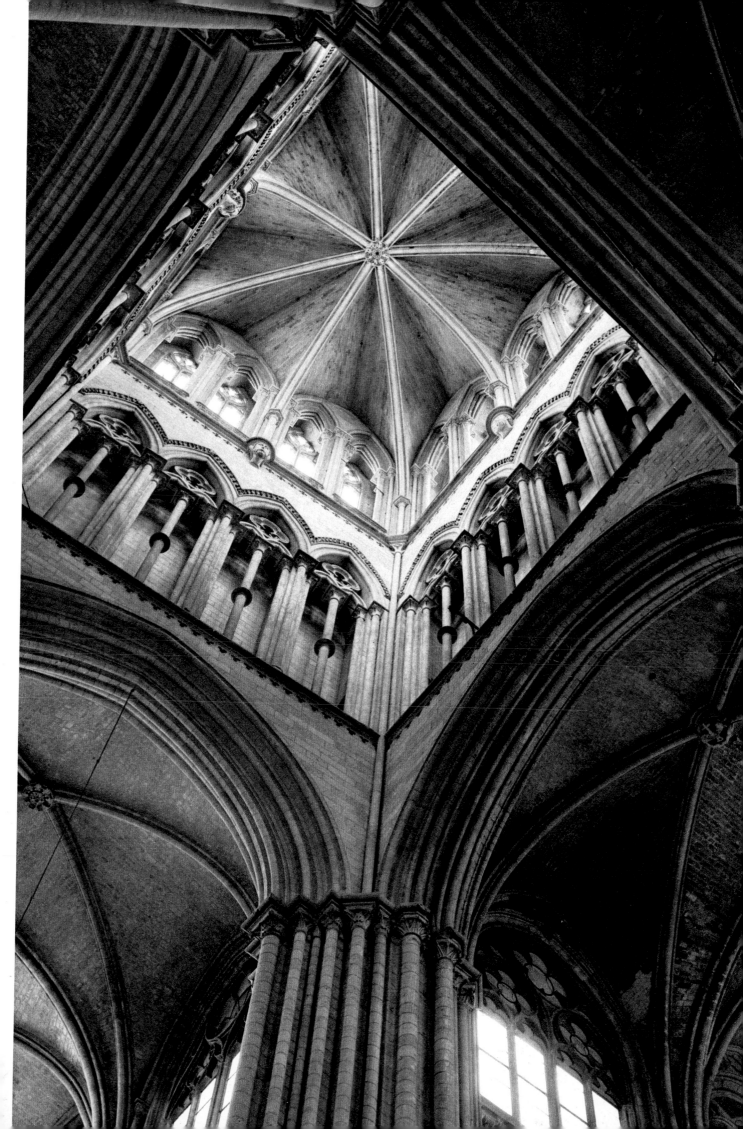

142-143 SÉES

145 BAYEUX 143

146–149 COUTANCES

150–151 LE MANS

154

155

156

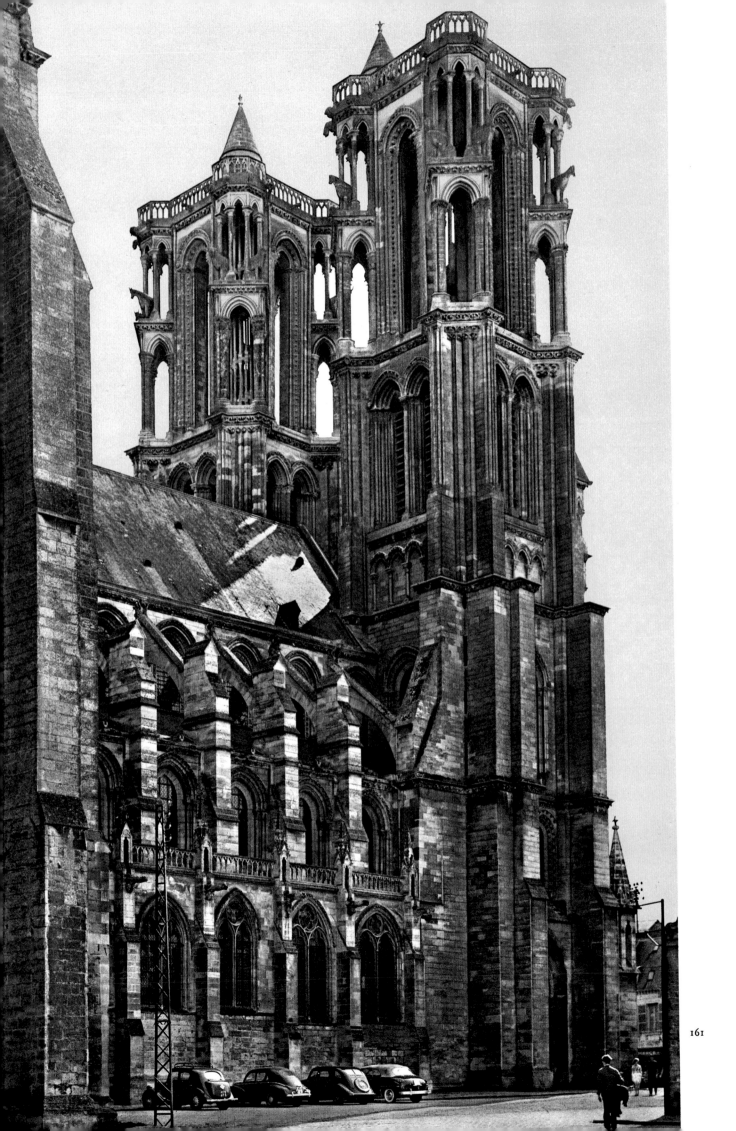

162

163

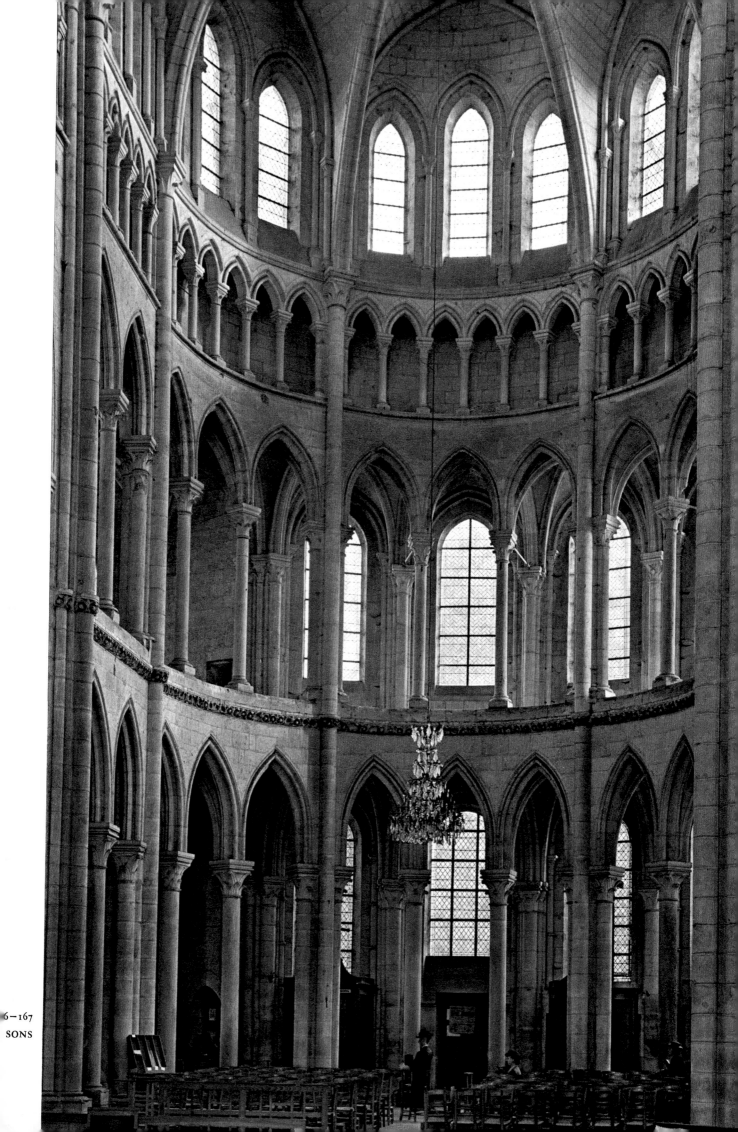

THE cathedral of St Stephen was begun in 1195 under Bishop Henri de Sully (1184–1199), brother of Eude de Sully, Bishop of Paris. The choir was finished in 1218, the nave in 1260.

Bourges Cathedral, like Notre-Dame in Paris, has a double aisle on either side of the nave and a rounded apse of archaic design, but possesses no transept. The little projecting chapels set all around the choir are unlike those of any other cathedral. An extensive crypt with Gothic vaults lies beneath the choir: it was built to correct the sloping site, not for any specific liturgical reasons.

The cathedral derives its fame mainly from the arrangement of the nave and aisles. Imagine a cathedral like Notre-Dame, with a double aisle surmounted by galleries on either side of the nave, in which the vaults of the inner aisles have been raised to those of the galleries, and you will have a picture of Bourges Cathedral. Envisage, furthermore, piers more than 55 feet high (as compared with the 21 feet of Notre-Dame in Paris) supporting the arcades of the nave, and you will appreciate the overwhelming effect of the interior. Bourges cathedral has influenced many later churches: in France, Le Mans and Coutances (east ends only); in Spain, Burgos, Toledo, Gerona, and Barcelona, all of which differ in details.

Colour Plate II (p. 27). Three windows from one of the small chapels projecting from the choir.

Colour Plate III (p. 37). Detail of one of the windows in the apse showing the story of the Prodigal Son and hunting scenes.

Colour Plate VIII (p. 227). A window in the apse with scenes from various legends.

171

The west front, characterized more by the vastness of its dimensions than by the harmony of the ensemble. The oldest portions of the cathedral are the two porches on the right and the left-hand one next to the central porch: all three date from *c.* 1250–1260. The central porch ('Portal of the Last Judgment') is only slightly later, *c.* 1260–1270. As for the porch on the extreme left, it is Late Gothic, having been built between 1513 and 1515, after the collapse of the northern parts of the façade in 1506. These five porches offer an interesting comparison of styles, the older ones having steep and relatively narrow gables, those on the left the rich openwork which is characteristic of Late Gothic.

The steps date from 1852.

172–173

Upper part of the central portal, 1270–1280, showing the Last Judgment. Plate 172 shows a detail of Christ enthroned displaying his wounds and flanked by four angels holding the instruments of the Passion; to the left and right of them are Mary and John kneeling in prayer; above are two more angels holding the sun and the moon. The second tier shows the Resurrected, naked figures portrayed with astonishing skill, rising from their graves. In the middle is St Michael weighing souls (Plate 173); left, Abraham under a canopy, with the Blessed; right, the Damned. The ~~voussures~~ *archivolts* show angels and saints.

174

The portals of the west front (cf. note to Plate 171). The great west window ('Le Grand Housteau') dates from 1390; in it rose window and traceried vertical windows are combined.

175–176

Arcading from the socles of the main portal. Above, the story of Noah, a superb example of leaf work, *c.* 1260–1270; below, Noah, his family and the animals entering the ark.

177

Three statues from the south porch. Moses, with the Tablets of the Law, is on the right. The south doorway with these elaborately carved archaic figures (*c.* 1160–1170) was included in the second stage of building which took place after 1225.

178

Statue of St Stephen at the south-west corner of the south portico; late thirteenth century.

179

Oblique view across the nave and into the double aisle on the north side. The nave is about 46 feet wide and 122 feet high. The inner aisles are 70, the outer aisles 30 feet high. The enormous piers rise to 56 feet before the arches begin—which exceeds the height of an ordinary four-storeyed building.

180

The choir seen from the east. The small chapels radiating from it are peculiar to this cathedral.

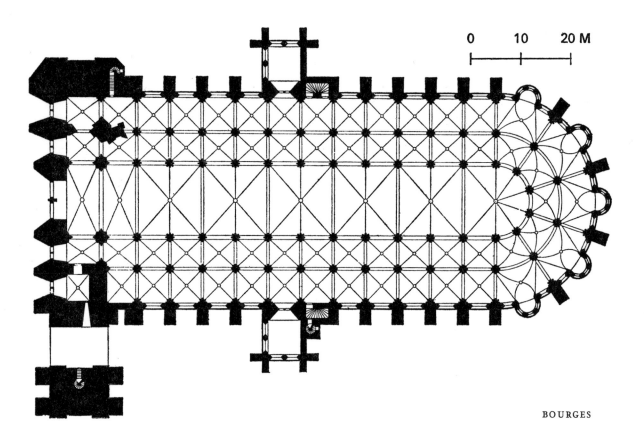

0   10   20 M

BOURGES

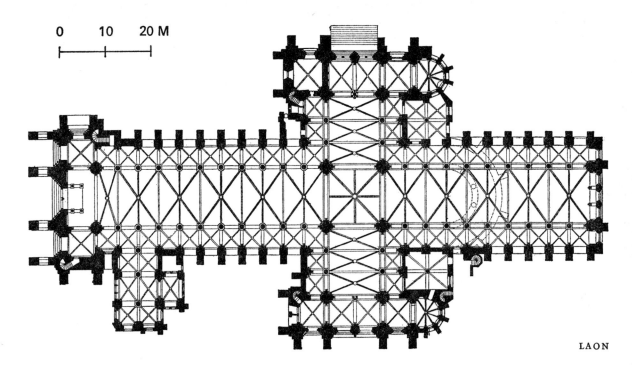

0 10 20 M

LAON

For notes see Page 175

172

175

176

STRASBOURG Plates 181–189

begun in 1015, was ome Romanesque) was re-used in the ved. Between 1175 septs were built on transept, the more ier decorated with : nave was rebuilt (1240–12, a the pure *rayonnant* style, and though wider, its design was based on the choir of Troyes and the nave of St Denis, the construction of which was still in progress. The unique façade was begun in 1276 and, after several changes of plan, it was completed in 1365 as a two-tower façade. A more ambitious scheme was then decided upon, and Ulrich of Ensingen built the octagonal portion of the north tower (1399–1419); the spire was built by Johannes Hültz between 1420 and 1439, and the tower, 466 feet high, became an object of universal wonder. In 1793 the cathedral was threatened with destruction by the Convention.

Colour Plate IX (p. 233). Statues representing prophets; from the right jamb of the main doorway of Strasbourg Cathedral.

181

The cathedral from the north-west. The intention was to have a gable over the rose window and then two freestanding towers. The original plans for the façade, drawn on parchment, have survived. On the left are the Romanesque choir and north transept.

182

The façade from the Kramgasse, which follows a Roman road leading to one of the former city gates. This medieval site was fortunately spared by nine-teenth-century developers, but one has to imagine the thirteenth-century houses as being much lower.

183

Right-hand portal of the west front. On the left, the Tempter and the World; on the right, three Foolish Virgins; below, the four seasons. Some of these statues are modern copies, the originals of which are in the 'Musée de l'Œuvre Notre-Dame'.

184

Two prophets from the left jamb of the main doorway, *c.* 1310–1320.

185

One of the Foolish Virgins from Plate 183.

186

The tympanum of the left doorway of the south transept: death of the Virgin. Christ has received her soul, which is represented as a small praying figure, *c.* 1230–1240.

187

Left-hand jamb of the left portal of the west front: Virtues overcoming Vices, before 1298.

188

A figure representing the vanquished Synagogue, on the right side of the double doorway of the south transept. The statue is a modern copy of an original dating from *c.* 1230–1240, now kept in the 'Musée de l'Œuvre'.

189

This pier (*c.* 1225–1230) with its decorative angels is unique in that it is used to support the four bays of the vault of the south transept.

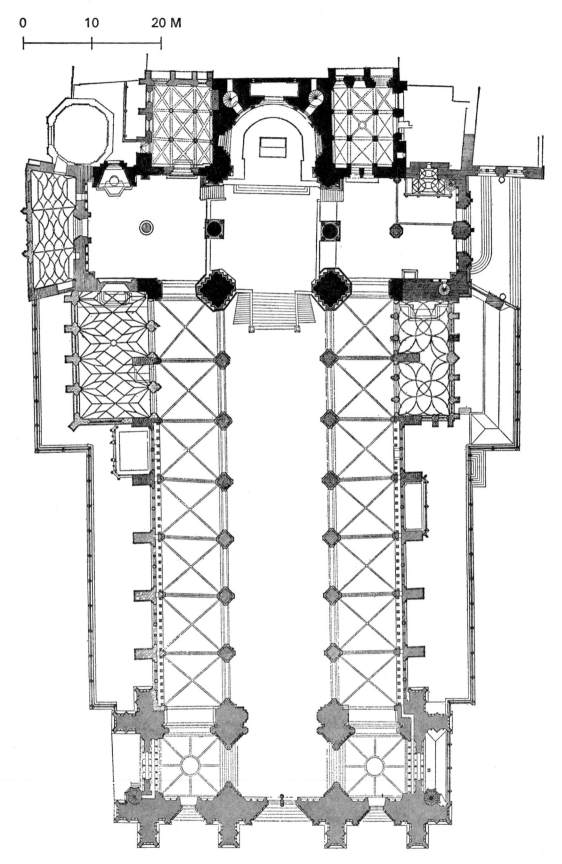

STRASBOURG